MYTH OF THE *Perfect* MOTHER

Kimberley Converse
AND
Richard Hagstrom

HARVEST HOUSE PUBLISHERS
EUGENE, OREGON 97402

Produced with the assistance of The Livingstone Corporation Carol Stream, IL 60188.

The Myth of the Perfect Mother

Copyright © 1993 by Harvest House Publishers
Eugene, Oregon 97402

Library of Congress Cataloging-in-Publication Data

Converse, Kimberley, 1960-
       The myth of the perfect mother / Kimberley Converse with
Richard G. Hagstrom.
           p.   cm.
       Includes index.
       ISBN 1-56507-076-3
       1. Motherhood—United States. 2. Mothers—United States. 3. Motherhood—
Religious aspects—Christianity. I. Hagstrom, Richard G. II. Title.
HQ759.C726   1993
306.874'3—dc20   92-25914
                                                                        CIP

*I dedicate this book to Mothers of Miracles (MOMs),
my mothers' support group. I've crossed paths with many
women through this group, as we've shared common struggles,
solutions, and dreams. The MOMs leadership group
has taught me much about teamwork, love,
serving, and being real. And all of the books we've
discussed together have contributed to the sensitivity and scope of*
The Myth of the Perfect Mother.

Contents

Part Six:
Maintaining Realistic Expectations
by Saying No

Part Seven:
Maintaining Realistic Expectations
Through Balance

Part Eight:
Reviewing Realistic Expectations

Part Nine

Acknowledgments

I owe my gratitude to the following people. . . .

Six years before I began to write *The Myth of the Perfect Mother*, Richard Hagstrom germinated the idea for it as he mentored me in his career counseling principles. It was my privilege to work with Richard.

I certainly never could have imagined how my life would not only be enriched but also challenged as I entered marriage and then parenthood. I must thank my husband, Dave, and my children Hannah and Nathan for allowing me to write about our family life, sometimes in not so glowing terms. And I am grateful to my sister, Lori Ferris, for her loving child care, freeing me up to write.

My husband was the first to read the rough draft. His comments, insights, and irenic spirit greatly shaped the tone of this book. I am indebted to Patricia Leal Welch whose thorough editing not only improved the manuscript, but also prompted me anew to be concerned about the details. Also, I thank others who supported me—Sue Poulin, Nan Lingenfelter, Suzanne Kum, Paul and Trish Kozlowski, and Al Converse.

The Livingstone Corporation embraced this project enthusiastically and wholeheartedly, envisioning the potential of the manuscript. Then Bruce Barton, Jim Galvin, Dave Veerman, and Daryl Lucas spent their talents and energies making it into the book that both they and I envisioned.

My writer's group, Scribes and Scribblers, provided me with the best training and encouragement that a new writer could hope for. Thanks to the leaders—Barbara Robidoux, Elisabeth Buddington, and Joan Coombs—as they "held their breath with me" while I awaited the word of acceptance from the publisher.

My publisher, Harvest House, took a chance on this first time writer, for which I am grateful. I'm pleased that Eileen Mason shared the same dream as mine—encouraging and helping moms by valuing their uniqueness.

PART ONE

Unrealistic Expectations on Moms

Chapter 1

The Myth of the Perfect Mother

◆

"Sorry I'm late," Ida apologized as she unbundled John and retrieved her other child's coat from the floor. "It was tough getting out the door." Ida gave her son a quick hug and sent him to play in the next room. The other moms, Rachael, Liz, and Tess, were already comfortably settled in for play group.

"John is entrenched in the terrible twos," Ida added as she removed her own coat. "He's got to do everything by himself. All I hear is, 'By self, by self, by self.' And when he doesn't get his way he throws a tem—"

"Mom, button for me," Amy interrupted as she handed Liz a doll.

Ida sat on the carpeted floor and continued with, "Yesterday I reminded John not to play with the candy at the checkout aisle. He did, so I tapped him on the hand.

He howled as if he'd been beaten. An older couple in line looked at me like I was an awful mom."

"I wish people could remember what it was like when their kids were little. Kids aren't little adults," stated Tess while bouncing Trevor on her knee.

"Someone should tell that to my husband. He's still not used to being interrupted in mid-sentence or used to the house not always being clean and orderly. He wanted me to develop a system for my cleaning," Ida sighed.

"Lauren spit up," Tess informed the group. As Rachael wiped Lauren's face and her own pants she listened attentively to the rest of the conversation.

"You're not that rigid," Liz said encouragingly. "No offense, but it's just not you." Liz thought of all that Ida enjoyed doing—the reading, the baking, the sewing, and the writing.

"I like a housecleaning system. It keeps me organized and on top of the situation," said Tess, "but it still doesn't stay clean very long. What really bothers me," she confided, "is the lack of quiet time to sit and think. Some days I feel smothered by the kids."

"Speaking of kids, Stacy's kids are here, but where is she?" asked Ida.

"Oh, I picked up her kids for play group so that she could nap. She overloaded her schedule and ended up at the emergency room at two in the morning with a severe migraine again," Liz explained.

Rachael had remained quiet. She wondered why Ida complained so much, why Tess wanted so much time to herself, and why Stacy did too many activities. She still liked them and considered them her friends. But she also felt she was different from them. *I enjoy spending time with my kids and I have a good relationship with my husband*, Rachael thought. *Housework—well, that's another—*

Rachael's thoughts were interrupted by the urgent pleadings of two children, each grabbing one end of a stuffed animal. And so goes a typical play group, where moms exchange complaints, observations, and each other's companionship.

Is today's generation any different from past generations? In a lot of ways it is; this generation has a whole arsenal of high tech innovations to help them, including more absorbent diapers, safer toys, and many more books. But in at least one way this generation of moms is just like our parents': Moms are still expected to be perfect. The pressure comes from many sources, and each puts its own spin on the "perfect mother" image. But no matter what the source, just about every mother feels it.

Perfect Mother:
Getting to Know Her

Just what is Perfect Mother like? Here's what I've learned about her. For starters, she remains calm and in control, even when the children act like little monsters. When she disciplines her kids it's always in love, and while she is firm she never raises her voice. Also, the perfect mom is fun-loving with her children. She's the kind of mom who lets her children miss school for a day so the family can go skiing, and who lets them eat dessert before dinner on special days. Her fun-lovingness carries over into her relationships with her many friends whom she invites over for parties and get-togethers. The perfect mom is hospitable and invites people over for dinner parties, making elaborate preparations and being gracious to her guests in meeting their needs.

On top of all this the perfect mom likes to do crafts

and can make all sorts of knickknacks so that her house is cleverly decorated. She sews her own curtains, designs her own stencils, and designs and sews her own clothes. She not only saves money but has gorgeous workmanship to show for her labors. The perfect mother works outside of the home two or three times a week to bring in extra money for the new car and because she likes to get out of the house to stimulate herself mentally. Her house is always freshly vacuumed. There is no clutter anywhere, her closets and drawers are organized, and she always knows where everything is.

Furthermore, she volunteers for activities in her community, church, and children's schools. She doesn't complain about money (or, for that matter, about anything). She's always attentive to the needs of her children, taking them to classes to develop their potential, driving them to school, knowing their friends, and being available to talk to after school. She makes perfectly well-balanced meals, but doesn't eat them, to keep her weight down. To maintain her own health, she jogs.

And then there's the whole area of her husband. She highly respects him. She makes sure his needs for time alone, privacy, and other activities are met. She is always available to listen to him and to encourage him. She takes time to look attractive and to set aside time for date nights and sex. She keeps up on current events in her community, her country, and the world. Sometimes she reads a fiction book for fun and to soak in the flavor of language itself.

Those are my images of that horrendously fictitious creature, Perfect Mother. She also goes by the less intimidating name of Good Mother. But by any name, she is the enemy.

Where the Myth of the Perfect Mother Comes From

We'd all like to be perfect. The only trouble with Perfect Mother is that she just doesn't exist. She doesn't now, she never did in the past, and she never will. And yet she lives among us, haunting us with her standards. I see her, as perhaps you do, and am compared to her in all kinds of ways.

TV and Movies

The Perfect Mother appears on television every week, on a popular show most famous for her funny husband (a doctor). This lawyer supermom has five well-behaved children. She and her husband spend time with the children, spend time with each other, volunteer in their community, exercise regularly, and have dinner guests over frequently. In addition, though there is no sign of a housekeeper or cook, her home is spotless, well-decorated, clutterless, and could be in any *House Beautiful* magazine.

For those moms who choose to deviate from that ideal by working at home instead of for a paycheck, the media's images are neither pretty nor flattering. In the most obvious example I can think of, the mother is lazy and does nothing but eat bonbons, shop, spend money, and feed off of soap operas. This show implies (incorrectly) that time spent being a homemaker is a waste. Still another series, long since canceled, would have you believe that as a wife and a mother you are no better than a slave. You are subservient to your husband because your brain no longer functions.

Comparing yourself with fiction and make-believe is about as fruitful as wishing you were Cinderella and your prince were just around the corner. Perfect Mother shows up on television and in the movies, but it's not playing at my house and I bet it's not playing at your house either. As a mom you need to set your sights on the reality around you and find a way to handle your individual situation effectively.

Your Mother

I love to hear basketball and football players talk about their mothers. In a typical rhapsody, the guy cannot say enough good about his mom. She's a saint. From the way he talks, you'd think that the only reason he made it into adulthood was because of his mother. He is in love with her; she has a special place in his heart forever. I've heard other athletes give similarly glowing reports about their moms.

I'm happy for those guys. And if you've had a great mom, you too can be thankful for all that she has given you.

But if you are a woman, there is a downside to having had a fantastic mom or idealizing your mom. You may expect yourself to be like her. She may have been well-suited for the roles of wife, mom, and homemaker. But you are a different woman from her. Do you have high expectations for yourself because of what your mom did right?

Extended family

Still another source of comparison is your own family, where you feel the pressure to comply with your parents' or your husband's parents' wishes (not to mention grandmother, sisters, or sisters-in-law). You may be told of how they handled such and such a crisis and how they raised their children. They can hardly camouflage their disappointment if you do not follow their advice about raising children. Occasionally we can be told,

"Well, it was good enough for our kids," when we want to do something different for our children.

But you have a unique family. Your family's makeup, with all of its individual personalities, is not like your or your husband's family growing up. As a new family you need to carve out your own identity based on who the people in it are. You, not your parents or your husband's parents, need to decide how to parent. Parents can offer advice and wisdom that should be sifted to glean what is appropriate to your family, to your lifestyle, and to your values. And certainly they want the best for you, for your spouse, and for your children. But they don't know the ins and outs of your days. Most importantly, you will have to deal diplomatically with each of your families. And that can be a real challenge.

In short, extended family have their own set of expectations for you. The trouble is, only some of their tricks and techniques will work well for you. Some may be good but difficult for you to use. Many will need to be exchanged for ways that better match your unique family.

Other Moms

Mothers often pass the Perfect Mother virus to each other. I still pick up the clutter before someone comes to visit, and I know that a lot of moms de-clutter their houses before I come over. I'm quick to share examples from how I handle my children, and what I've accomplished in other areas of my life. Yet I hesitate to tell of the lemon meringue pies that had to be eaten with spoons. I don't tell about running out of the house at 9:45 P.M. before the store closes to buy one ingredient I forgot to buy for the dessert I have to make tonight for tomorrow's lunch.

Perhaps as mothers we should be more realistic, more understanding, and kinder concerning the struggles we all share. Perhaps instead of giving advice we should merely say, "Yes, I know what that's like." Maybe we should often just listen and not give any advice.

Comparing yourself with other moms leads to unrealistic expectations of what you are able to do. The Perfect Mother I imagine tends to be a combination of the traits that I admire in my friends and acquaintances in how they handle their many roles. If only I could be in control like my friend Pam, whom I've never heard raise her voice (and Pam has five children). If only I could be more fun-loving like Nan, more hospitable like Arva, more creative and hands-on like Margot, more organized and clean like Trish, more involved in volunteer activities like Sue, more into kids' classes and needs like Chris, more frugal and practical like Deb, and more admiring of my husband like Sue.

Yet the world is made up of "what are's," not "if only's." I'm sure you know women like Pam, Nan, Arva, Margot, Trish, Sue, Chris, and Deb whom you admire and emulate in certain ways. And it's fine to admire them. But don't expect yourself to become like them. You are projecting their strengths onto your weaknesses. Such comparisons only lead to frustration and envy.

My friends admire me too, but for different reasons. I make up my own recipes, take my kids to libraries and museums, and refinish, fix, and redecorate furniture. I also like to research information and express my thoughts through writing. Undoubtedly your friends admire your positive qualities and want to be like you in those areas. They also admire when you admit your weaknesses and share your struggles; they admire you for your honesty.

We are all different from one another. We each have our strengths as well as our weaknesses. And because of this we have trade-offs. My fun-loving friends tend to be terrible budgeters and spend money quickly. I tend to be more serious and less fun-loving, yet good with money. None of us is perfect and we have to accept both our strengths and weaknesses.

If you're still wondering if you have any strengths after reading about some of the talented people I know, let me assure you that you do. The next chapter will show you how you can pinpoint those strengths.

You may know a mom who appears to have glided into the job of motherhood. She is not able to tell you how she fits into it so easily; she is not able to tell you that maybe accidentally she has found her niche in mothering. Instead she may tell you what works for her and her family. But because you are different from her, her advice and help may only frustrate you. You may think, *She makes it look so easy! It works for her; why doesn't it work for me?* Women who "make it look easy" have customized motherhood to who they are, and often think that what works for their family will work for others. It doesn't. You have to make your own fit.

Meddlers

Perfect Mother haunts you most when you're out in public. Strangers who don't have kids or don't remember what it's like to have kids are usually responsible for conjuring her image. You know the scene: As you do your best to check out your library books or get all the items on your grocery list, the kids are screaming or whining or throwing temper tantrums, when suddenly these people appear out of nowhere. As you struggle to juggle the kids and their many demands, the meddlers shake their heads and whisper (or, rudest of all, say to you directly) something like, "I wouldn't let my kids do that if I were their mother." Such people can cause mothers to question their performance; after all, "How can I be a good mother if I can't control my children?"

You are virtually guaranteed to hear meddlers question your parenting. Some strangers may make you feel that there must be some Perfect Mother out there who doesn't let their kids "misbehave" in public. But I don't know where she is, do you? My kids are real and they get fussy and cry and most of all act like children. And they don't put on a face for people in public.

Peer Groups

A peer group could include just about any group or association that you belong to formally or informally—your neighborhood, church, friends, social club, co-workers, husband's co-workers, mother's support group, or professional society. These peer groups have a big influence on how you and your family behave because you value these groups and wish to remain a part of them.

A peer group may have a set agenda for how women should behave in general and may specifically tell you that you should behave this way also. As a member of a women's group you may be expected to carry a full-time job in addition to being a mom. As a member of a church organization it may be frowned upon if you work full-time outside of the home. Peer groups can be a powerful influence in your lifestyle choices.

Husbands

My husband, Dave, has thoughts on what I should be like and how the kids should behave. He has standards for how he'd like the house to look and for how the kids should behave. But sometimes I don't think he realizes my reality as a mom. He's at the office all day. He doesn't know the seemingly constant battles, care, and work that go along with caring for children and keeping a household. Nor will he probably ever, even though he tells me sometimes, "They're my kids too," or, "I take care of them too." I have to face the fact that we are in two separate worlds until he comes home from work. Once he's home, I feel it's my job to train him by bringing other families over for dinner or get-together time. This gives him a chance to see how other kids misbehave and act up. Then I hear him say, "Oh, now I see—it's a stage," or, "Oh, other kids do that too."

My husband's expectations for me are often based on what his own mother did and did not do. Dave's mom didn't go overboard on cleaning her house, so I'm off the hook on that one. However, she is an avid saver and I'm not. This area has been a source of conflict for us.

My fantasy is to leave home for a week to go off and do concentrated research and writing, leaving Dave home with the kids, the cooking, and the laundry. Then he'd have more than just head knowledge of this mother-hood job—he'd have practical experience. Through this experience I think Dave would really learn what kids are like, what juggling a house is all about, and how boring it can be to plan and make three meals a day. Then I think some of his expectations for the perfect mother, wife, and lover would change for the better.

In balance, Dave is also my helper, friend, and confidant. He is the one who can give me insights into myself and the kids because, as a mom, I am often too close to the chaos to see clearly. Often my husband's objective input is valuable in solving problems or in averting problems before they start. In parenting, as in other aspects of our marriage, we need to practice teamwork because each of us brings valuable resources to the tough job of parenting.

Children

One day my daughter said to me out of the blue,

"Mother, were you thinking that I was bored?" From a very early age (my daughter was three at the time), children assume that mom thinks only about them. Meanwhile, a lot of times as mothers our minds are often on our children. At times I've thought, *Uh oh, I don't hear any noise,* or, *Uh oh, I hear too much noise.* I wonder if their needs are being met for food, vitamins, and good clothes. I ponder whether I have bought the right toys for them, played with them enough, or disciplined them properly.

Children place great demands on moms. Some of these demands you will need to meet and others you will have to meet in other ways (preschool, day camp, or extra activities). Each child is different with the time they need to be with parents. Though you have to accommodate your children, you cannot let them set the pace entirely.

Frenzied Lifestyle

Our culture has raised running around to an art form. Many mothers are locked into a constant cycle of packing the car, loading in the kids, and driving to birthday parties, preschool, play groups, dance lessons, soccer, and lunches at the drive-through. Why? Perfect Mothers go places, no matter how much havoc it wreaks on their schedule. At the end of the day they are tired and worn out and wonder, "Is this the way to be a mom?" The unwritten answer is yes.

We are the minivan generation; our lives are not geared around our neighborhood as our moms' lives were. Rather, our day is spent partly at home and partly in a whirlwind of going to this or that event, place, or lesson. The belief that we are doing this for our children's sake only makes it harder to slow down. But is that the way for everyone to be a mom?

The Mythical Ideal

The mythical ideal is that motherhood is baking cookies and sharing tender moments and being your child's best friend and always knowing the right thing to do. It's a baby's soft skin or cuddling on the couch while reading a book or happy memories all of the time. Many moms harbor this mythical image in their idealistic imagination. Perhaps you do too.

Yet motherhood is seldom like the mythical idea. It would help to look at motherhood as something other than mystical. It would help to look at motherhood for what it is, a job comprised of many responsibilities. If motherhood could be looked at like a job, then perhaps some of the perfectionist images could be altered.

A Composite

Your image of the Perfect Mother is a composite of what you've seen around you in your friends, your mother, your acquaintances, on TV shows, and in society. Your mind has rolled all of these expectations into one grand Perfect Mother against whom you continually compare yourself.

Images of the Perfect Mother may spur you on to try harder and achieve more. Sometimes you can trick yourself into believing that if you only try harder you can be that person. But usually that type of trying leads mainly to frustration and stress, not to becoming a better mother.

The problem is that you cannot live up to a Perfect Mother constructed from all the expectations placed on you by society, friends, husbands, children, or even by you yourself. And you shouldn't *try*. Yet, "inwardly women still feel trapped by a deep conviction that their lives are only on loan to them, borrowed from creditors, all those external arbiters who set the standard for the goodness and to whom they feel responsible."[1]

A Plan of Action

What are you to do about the unrealistic expectations placed on you as a mother? First and foremost is to knock some of those perfect images out of your head. If the Perfect Mother movie continually plays in your head and you're not meeting that image, you will constantly strive and always be frustrated. Keep only the images that help you.

Second, you need to evaluate the validity of the expectations placed on you by others; to ask whether these expectations are realistic, and whether the people who impose them on you are looking out for their own interests or yours. You may also want to evaluate why the people and groups who influence you have such a powerful effect.

Lingering Doubts

You may have nagging questions and doubts about being a mother. Perhaps you've felt more disappointment than joy and bonding as a mother. Perhaps you felt that when you gave birth, supermom hormone would spew into your body and magically transform you into Mom Capable. Maybe you thought you'd suddenly love to cook and clean or at least love to be with your children all day long. You may have thought motherhood would be natural. And perhaps now you are surprised to find most of your expectations shattered.

In any event, you don't fit the picture of the Perfect Mother. Perhaps you don't like cooking or cross-stitch. Maybe you even yell at your kids whom you love so much. And so you feel guilty for not always liking or enjoying many of the things that mothers are supposed to love to do. What are you supposed to base your expectations on? What should be your performance standards for you as a mom?

Expectations placed on you to be the perfect mother are frustrating, stressful, and unattainable. Are you tired of perfect standards and idyllic images? I was too! No mother can be perfect because every mother is *unique*—and that is the key to breaking free from the Myth. We'll begin to find out how in the next chapter.

Chapter 2

Every Mother Is Unique

———————◆———————

"I have nothing to wear," I whined to myself. I felt like the ungrateful stepsisters in *Cinderella* who discarded perfectly good clothes and grumbled that other people always owned better clothing. Yet I had spent half an hour trying on various combinations of clothing and none had been to my liking. Some were too tight in the hips, others didn't match, and still others were outdated. We were already ten minutes late for a wedding and I was still in my slip. I had enough clothes; there were piles of them on the bed, the floor, and the dresser. Still I struggled to find the right outfit. I forced myself into something and remained uncomfortable all day. And my husband, Dave, had trouble understanding why I had such difficulty in, of all things, dressing myself.

I had a lot of clothes in my closet. Yet each time I needed something to wear, I struggled to find the right outfit. I had many colors, many styles, various levels of dressiness and, most of all, many sizes from which to choose. But after having two kids my body had changed size, shape, and weight. My frustration grew until I decided it was time to consolidate my wardrobe.

I agonized for hours sorting my clothes into piles and deciding which ones to keep. With resolve I scooped up all the clothes that used to fit, put them into a black 40-gallon trash bag, and gave them away. In another 40-gallon bag I deposited the pile of older clothes that were worn out or were out of style. The attic became home for the clothes that I really love and hate to part with, such as good suits and nice dresses. I put the clothes that needed sewing or mending in my sewing dresser. Lastly, I placed the remaining good clothes in my closet, disappointed that there were so few left. No wonder I had such difficulty deciding what to wear.

Pregnancy had done a job on my body. Yet I had clung to my clothes thinking that maybe someday they would fit. Perhaps they would have—some day. But in the process I had been frustrating myself and complicating my life. I had never been the perfect *Cosmopolitan* shape, and any hope of looking exactly like that were disappearing. Cleaning my closet freed me up; I had let go of the myth of the perfect body!

If the Shoe Doesn't Fit...

Becoming a mother brings changes that are difficult for many women to accept. Just as you may refuse to acknowledge the changes in your body after giving birth, you may refuse to acknowledge the fact that the very fabric of your life has changed. After all, how could one little baby cause so much change? And if you do admit the changes, you may be at a loss, at least initially, to know how to handle the transition.

What role should a new mother step into? There are so many options and choices. The world, through the media (television in particular), holds out many possibilities. And then you look (naturally) to your mother, grandmother, peer groups, and other mothers to try to figure out motherhood. But then many options disappear when you consider your style, personal preferences, and family's needs. You can find yourself thinking, *Why does motherhood feel so awkward?* As a woman, you may feel as if you are in a bind because mothering does not fit you, yet the old life doesn't fit either; neither one is comfortable, neither life fits. At first that seems discouraging, but it doesn't have to be.

Like the clothes in my closet, not all the roles, styles, and options available to moms are right for me—or you. We must eliminate and concentrate our lifestyle wardrobes so that they fit us. And that starts with knowing how we are designed, what our strengths are, and what fits each of us.

That process must start with you. As with clothes, you need to decide your size, your style, and your good colors, and put them together so that the combination works.

. . . Maybe You Need a New Pair

"I always wanted to be a mom but I'm disappointed that it's so hard," a friend lamented in my play group. Many of us nodded in silent agreement. This silence spoke volumes as we each privately reviewed the demands of mothering that had surprised us.

Perhaps you have felt like that. Mothering is hard work. But you can make it harder—as many women do—by trying to live up to perfect (artificial) standards and idyllic images. Most women have unrealistic expectations about how to be a mom. As one mom wrote, "So many people have *unrealistic expectations,* and then reality appears especially hard."[1] We need to give ourselves some tender loving care in the job of mothering. What moms need is specific help instead of perfect standards and idyllic images.

...Tailored to Fit You

The main message I want you to catch from this book is that *the responsibilities of motherhood can and should be tailored to your intrinsic design as a woman.* This will reduce stress, guilt, inappropriate "ought's," and frustration in mothering—in effect, providing care for you as a caregiver. Eventually, most moms find out what works for them by luck anyway—and with a lot of unnecessary frustration and guilt. As you'll soon see, it needn't be that way.

The tack we'll take is to apply career counseling techniques to your job of mothering. Together we'll evaluate the jobs, roles, and tasks involved in motherhood and help you tailor the responsibility to fit you. After all, motherhood is not what the books say, not what you thought it was before you had children, and not how society defines it. Motherhood is how *you* define it and what you choose to make it. Therefore, you should strive to fit the role and tasks of mothering to the needs of you and your family.

See the Light, the Green Light

The Green Light Concept (GLC) was developed by Richard G. Hagstrom. From thousands of interviews with people, he found out what makes people unique and, therefore, what jobs suit each one. There are four Green Focus areas in the GLC model. You are strongest in one of these; this is your personal Green Focus area and a description of your greatest strengths. You will have another focus that is somewhat strong for you, your Yellow Focus area. Together these two combine to form your Green Light Profile.

The Green Light Concept helps a woman see that she has a particular design that influences what she likes to do and does well. For example, my Green Focus area is the world of Ideas. Knowing my design has alleviated stress in my life and allowed me to set my own standards instead of those set by others. I am free to make individual decisions based on my Green Light Profile. From these decisions I can set realistic expectations for myself.

The Green Light Concept

Your personal Green Light profile is made of:
- your Green Focus area
- your Green Action Skills—skills you use when you are highly motivated

○ **Green**—your major life focus based on what you do well and find satisfying

○ **Yellow**—your minor life focus based on what you do well and find somewhat satisfying.

○ **Red**—tasks and roles you neither do particularly well nor find satisfying

© Hagstrom Consulting

For some women, the application of the Green Light Concept means altering their expectations of motherhood. Yet for others, GLC means not only altering their expectations but also taking on some new jobs or responsibilities that utilize strengths they had not been using before. In my case, I needed to work for pay part-time as well as volunteering. Though I love my husband and my children, I needed a source of additional fulfillment which resulted from using my Green strengths and skills. Tasks moms may need to begin a new hobby. Relationships moms may need to develop more relationships. And Strategy moms may need to oversee some process or group of people outside the home.

While bookstores are filled with "how to" books, guidebooks, cassette tapes, and videos for many kinds of jobs and careers, I have never seen any material that examines motherhood as a job and treats the mother as a skilled worker doing that job. While career men and women are encouraged to utilize their potential and to find a job that suits them, mothers' books emphasize the tasks that need to be done (such as housecleaning), and seemingly without regard for the design of the mother.

In fact, almost all books on parenting leave me with specific feelings after I've read them: either I'm overwhelmed with what they say I ought to be doing, or I'm perplexed by their vagueness and lack of solutions. After reading these books I feel like asking, "Is everyone the same, having the same needs and doing the same activities to meet these needs?" I don't think so.

Proceed with Realistic Expectations

With an emphatic burst I say, "We are each different in how we are made!" Each person has a unique design, and every mother has her own Green Focus area, personality, and set of Green Action Skills to be used in effective mothering. Realizing your personal strengths can rescue you from being deluded by the myth of the Perfect Mother.

By applying career counseling techniques to the job of motherhood, you will better realize that your work as a mother is valuable. One author wrote, "The glut of books on parenting seems to make things worse, for many postulate, often in a condescending tone, impossible ideals of parenthood, focusing on what we should do and be, instead of who we are."[2] *The Myth of the Perfect Mother* will help you escape from "impossible ideals of parenthood" so you can focus on the reality of who you are.

Here's how I'll proceed:

Part I—Unrealistic Expectations on Moms

Perfect Mother expectations can cause frustration and stress because many of those expectations are inappropriate for you. In these first two chapters I've described where Perfect Mother expectations come from and what's wrong with them.

Part II—Foundations for Realistic Expectations

Chapters Three and Four will help you identify your personal strengths and acknowledge your lifetime dreams. They are foundational in setting realistic expectations for yourself.

Part III—Setting Realistic Expectations in Family Relationships

The topic of Chapters Five, Six, and Seven is family. Your life is intertwined with others, especially family members. Each person in your family has his or her own dreams. Knowing that you are a team and that you have different abilities and personal strengths can make mothering easier and strengthen your family ties.

Part IV—Setting Realistic Expectations in Housework

In Chapter Eight I'll evaluate the job of maintaining a home in light of the four Green Focus areas. Determining your housecleaning standards and adjusting expectations for these time-consuming jobs may free some valuable time to pursue lifetime dreams or give you the encouragement to concentrate more effort on your home.

Part V—Setting Realistic Expectations in Work

In Chapters Nine and Ten you'll get a broad examination of the work options available to you, taking into consideration your Green Focus area, lifetime dreams, values, and lifestyle decisions.

Part VI—Maintaining Realistic Expectations by Saying No

By saying no to inappropriate options, your lifestyle will be filled with activities and opportunities that are suited to you. In Chapter Eleven I'll show how the measly word no can simplify your life and free up precious time for pursuing your lifetime dreams.

Part VII—Maintaining Realistic Expectations through Balance

You are more balanced when you establish and maintain your physical health and relationship with God. Chapters Twelve and Thirteen will help you maintain balance in those areas.

Part VIII—Reviewing Realistic Expectations

Your life is full of changes and options. You'll need to determine realistic expectations with each new season of mothering so you don't let perfectionism and unrealistic expectations run your life. In Chapter Fourteen, you'll get an opportunity to do that.

Contrary to popular belief, motherhood is a job. It is absolutely essential that you learn your areas of strength and weakness so you can adjust mothering to how God made you. I want you to be able to identify the sources of expectations in your life, to look at those desires for perfection in the light of your Green Light Profile, lifetime dreams, and values, and then carve out your own mothering niche.

Dispelling the Myth

Applying the Green Light Concept can help you as a mother:

- ♦ Accept your style and skills
- ♦ Set realistic expectations based on your style, skills, and levels of competence
- ♦ Adjust your responsibilities to fit your strengths
- ♦ Reduce frustration and stress
- ♦ Increase your confidence in your mothering abilities
- ♦ Strengthen your family ties

My intention is to help you be a mom in the '90s, with all its expectations, stresses, and many complications. It's a book that encourages you to look at who you are as a person and how this affects the way you rear your children. As you read, you will examine how you can be effective in many responsibilities based on who you are. The question is not, "Are you doing enough?" but, "Are you doing the right things based on your Green Focus area?" As a mother with two preschoolers I have very little free time, so I want to use it to its full advantage; I want to use my time doing what I enjoy and do well. By making such adjustments, I am able to recharge my batteries and rejuvenate myself.

Once you know who you are, you can make some adjustments to your lifestyle by setting realistic expectations. Sometimes that means you will lower your standards. (Some moms tell me if they lower their standards any more they'll be at zero!) In other areas you'll need to increase your standards. As you'll see later, though, accepting realistic expectations does not give you license to ignore responsibilities or not to work on improving your weak areas. It is merely a way to say, "I'm not good at such and such; when I do it too much I feel frustrated and bored, and I never do a good job at it."

I may sound confident in telling you all this. Do I have it all together? No. What I thought had been a relatively together life unraveled with the arrival of children. I struggled with motherhood and with my self-esteem. Through use of the Green Light Concept and the support of a local mother's group, I altered the job of motherhood to fit the person I am. Having found my balance for this season in my life, I'd like to help other moms achieve a working balance for their lives.

I have days of frustration, when I feel like screaming and wish I could stop being a mother for a while. I still dislike juggling schedules and running out of milk for morning cereal, bread for peanut butter and jelly sandwiches, or diapers for my little guy. I'm not a happy camper when my kids are sick, sick, and sick. I still over-schedule myself, feeling stressed out as I try to do too much.

But there are fewer days like that for me as I schedule and care for my children in light of my Green Light Profile. My esteem is out of the cellar now, in part because I have a sense of accomplishment. I raise my voice at my kids less often. And when I'm with them physically, I'm also with them mentally and emotionally because my batteries have been recharged. I use my strengths more and I understand why I feel drained when I can't!

So who am I that you should listen? I'm certainly not an expert. Rather, I'm a mom, just like you. A mom with a desire to help other women find their GLC mothering style to relieve some of the stresses and frustrations of motherhood. I want you to find your mothering niche. I don't do power lunches or satellite conferences or mega-meetings; I do "Happy Meals," potty training, and sleepless nights. And I write.

I didn't write this book because I have it all together. I wrote it because I wanted to share what has helped me. Moms need concrete help and encouragement, not mythical ideals. I also wrote it because gathering information and writing is part of my Green Light Profile; it's a strength of mine. (B.C.—before children—I did career counseling with Richard Hagstrom.) I don't have all the answers to your mothering dilemmas, just a message of hope.

HLP!

While in California I once saw a minivan with a license plate that read: "HLP5KDS." I understood immediately. I'm not sure what kind of help that mom wanted or needed, but I certainly understood her plea. After reading one too many of those self-help books that do a wonderful job of describing the stresses and frustrations of motherhood while offering little concrete help, it became my plea as well.

Do you compare yourself unfavorably to other moms? Do you think you have nothing unique to offer your children? Do you think your accomplishments look simple?

I'll repeat it again and again because it's central to the message of this book: You are not like any other mom. Understanding your Green Light Profile will help you know why you feel frustration with some aspects of motherhood and give you a way to handle your unpleasant responsibilities. In the next chapter you'll learn what makes you unique and what your strengths are.

PART TWO

Foundations for Realistic Expectations

Chapter 3

Mothering Styles

———◆———

Remember Alice in Walt Disney's *Alice in Wonderland*? Alice went through many changes entering wonderland and encountered many surprises. She became huge, then petite, then big again, and then small. She chased after a rabbit with a pocket watch, encountered a talking seagull, listened to flowers singing, and chatted with an obnoxiously arrogant caterpillar. After all she'd been through, the caterpillar constantly asked her, "Who are you?" Her head spun as she replied, "I hardly know, sir."[1]

Sometimes in the wonderland of motherhood (it's a wonder any of us make it through), I feel like Alice. Through pregnancies my body has gone to huge and back again and huge and back again. Sleepless nights, being on call 24 hours a day, mixed messages about motherhood—all of these factors wear down my sense of identity. Knowing what my strengths and weaknesses are has been a godsend.

Now let's spend some time finding out who you are.

Tales of Four Women

The school year is almost over, and it's time to plan summer vacations. As you read the stories of four moms and how they handled their vacation plans, note how they are different and which woman you most identify with.

Rachael's Reminder

Rachael flipped through a photo album containing shots of last year's family vacation. She smiled as the pictures stirred memories of a baby who couldn't yet walk, and (oh yes) how Rick's vocabulary at age three had really matured. A year had passed by quickly—too quickly—and it was time to think about this year's vacation.

Her husband Randy entered the room. "The kids have sure grown," he said as he glanced at the family shoot. "That was a great vacation."

"Yes it was. We had so much time together and had such fun," Rachael responded. "The kids are really getting close."

Rebecca, their oldest daughter said, "Fun, but a little disorganized. I mean, we forgot the towels and the silverware."

"Well that's what memories are made of," said Rachael wistfully. "The important thing is that we had lots of time to spend together. What do the two of you want to do for vacation this year?"

"The same place would be fine Mom. Only please remember the towels!"

"Hon, that same place would be great," added her husband.

She hoped the same cottage would be available, even though it was rather late to be planning. Rachael wondered where she had written down the phone number. She looked forward to spending time with her family again. These years were going by quickly, and she was really enjoying them.

Tess' Tale

Tess began her vacation plans many months ago. She prides herself in planning—"the key to a good vacation," she liked to say. After all, one can't leave things to chance; unexpected surprises tend to be unpleasant.

Tess sat down at her computer and called up the file for vacation. At the top of the list were "Economical Lodgings." There wasn't much money this year, so she and her husband had decided to rent a small, rustic housekeeping unit near a lake. That would save money, as she could cook many of their meals. They had also decided to go off-season to save more money. Thankfully, the kids were still preschoolers.

Next she looked at her projected budget for the vacation. She had categories for lodging, food, gas and tolls, amusements, laundry, and miscellaneous. She wondered if she had overlooked any expenses, but couldn't think of any.

She flipped down her file to find her packing list. She didn't want to forget anything. Tess had categories for hiking gear, bike rack and bikes, fishing gear, canoe and equipment, food, cooking supplies, dinnerware, car games and toys, towels, clothes, beach toys, board games, clothes, and cleaning supplies.

Satisfied that her list was complete, she moved on to her final listing. She compiled a list of last minute things to do. It read: Cancel paper, stop mail deliveries, have Tom (her husband) check the car thoroughly (tires, oil, lube, wheel alignment).

She would call the lake today to confirm their reservation. She looked forward to spending time with her family, and she didn't want any overlooked detail to spoil it.

Ida's Itinerary

Ida lamented the short amount of vacation time (one week) she had accumulated this past year. *There is so much to see and experience!* she thought.

She wished she had more time to learn and experience with the kids. Her children were aged three and six—some attention span but not much. Thus they were too young to spend a lengthy vacation in Washington, D.C. *Besides the cost would be too much this year—living on one small salary is tight. Perhaps when they are older . . .* Sturbridge Village was close and it would be a good learning experience. But then she thought better of it. *Too close. We can do that for a weekend trip.* She decided that Amish country would be good to spend at her relatives' house. Her sister had invited them down. The kids could see and experience a new lifestyle and the nature sights around were beautiful. If they wanted to they could go into Washington to get a taste of it for one day.

She made a mental note to remember to bring the camera, lenses, and plenty of film—the new sights and area would lend itself to some great scenic shots. Also, she'd like to bring her cross-stitch and lap quilt that she never seemed to have time to do. Maybe her sister could show her how to make reed baskets; she'd wanted to learn how to for a while. She reminded herself to bring some tapes for the kids, a book on tape for herself, and some soothing music tapes. She sighed, *I hope I have time to myself to think.*

Stacy's Story

Stacy looked at her pocket planner and found that it was time to make plans for the family's vacation. In her planner it read: "Call Mark, travel agent." His phone number was listed. She'd used the same agent for the past three years. It was a little more expensive, but he had done a good job and it beat sweating the details herself.

This year Shawn and the kids wanted to do a vacation like last year's, except they didn't have the funds to fly this year. In her planner she wrote, "Resort area within one day's drive, preferably less." She noted that the resort needed to have secretarial and fax services nearby—unfortunately she had a deadline for a project and would need to be available for consultation. She also noted: "Nearby mountain climbing and/or rappelling. Will need child care for the day!" Also, she wanted a place that offered a night out for the parents, to dine and see a play. There, that should do it!

Stacy picked up the phone, thinking about spending time as a family and having time to do something adventurous. But she hesitated to call. She almost wished that they could skip this year's vacation. She was solidly in the middle of work deadlines. But it would just be for one week . . .

Stacy dialed the travel agent's number, hoping he could meet her requirements.

Identifying Your Green Light Profile

Which of those women were you able to identify with most strongly? In terms of the Green Light Concept, Stacy is a Strategy person. She likes to plan strategy and to see results. If you identified with Stacy, your Green Focus area may be Strategy.

Tess is a Tasks person. She delights in doing tasks, being organized, and having all the details in place. If you identified with Tess, you may be a Tasks person.

Ida is an Ideas person. She has found her strengths to lie in conceptualizing, thinking, musing, and the like. She needs time alone to think. If you found yourself identifying with Ida, you too may be an Ideas person.

Rachael is a Relationships person. She delights most in being with people and in sharing experiences with them. If you identified most with Rachael, your Green may be Relationships.

Like those four moms, every mom has a Green Focus area—an area in which she thrives. You do too.

Take a look at the Green Focus Area Comparison Chart on page 47. The descriptions of Strategy, Tasks, Ideas, and Relationships Focus areas are typical for each of these groups. See if you can find the one that best describes you. That is your Green Focus area. The one that is next closest to fitting you is your Yellow. And the one that is least like you is your Red.

Understanding Your Green Light Profile

Your Green Light Profile is made up of your Green Focus area and your Yellow Focus area. It also involves knowing what is Red for you (the area or areas in which you do poorly). If you want to analyze your Focus areas a little more in depth, the chart "The ABCs of GLC" (pp. 57-59) will give you a little more information. Simply follow the instructions and tally the results. An even more extensive analysis involves listing and analyzing *positive experiences* you've had over the years. If you're

Green Focus Area Comparison Chart

	Strategy	Tasks	Ideas	Relationships
Will usually try to:	• Win • Come out ahead	• Do everything perfectly	• Understand everything, or come up with original ideas	• Help people • Befriend people
Key descriptive words:	• Pusher • Spearhead	• Plodder • Consistent	• Cerebral • Artist	• Socialite • Uplifter
Makes most decisions:	• Quickly • Decisively	• Slowly • Analytically	• Deliberately • Contemplatively	• By group consensus
Best with people as (role):	• Director • Promoter	• Project Controller • Troubleshooter	• Researcher • Designer/ Creator	• Spark plug, Encourager • Special helper, Facilitator

My Green Focus area is probably: _____

My Yellow Focus area is probably: _____

My Red Focus area is probably: _____

- ◆ **S** is for Strategy. A Strategy person is concerned with the bottom line—results—and the overall picture.
- ◆ **T** is for Tasks. A Tasks person enjoys the process of working with details to obtain some tangible outcome.
- ◆ **I** is for Ideas. An Ideas person thrives on using ideas creatively, either for the joy of learning or in creative, artistic expression.
- ◆ **R** is for Relationships. A Relationships person loves spending time with people; she is a "people person."

© Hagstrom Consulting

interested in doing a *Positive Experiences* listing, turn to Appendix G, which has a worksheet that will walk you through the process.

Applying Your Green Light Profile

You've determined your Green Focus area. Now comes the important part of applying it to your life.

From now on I'll use the words Strategy, Tasks, Ideas, and Relationships a lot. Remember which one is your Green and which one is your Yellow.

The whole point of identifying your Green Light Profile is so you can concentrate on using your Green and Yellow Focus areas while avoiding your Reds as much as possible. You'll get the most fulfillment from using your Green. The Green is important to life but it isn't your whole life. Spend some time on your Yellow, but not so much that you begin to dread doing activities in that category. The rest of the GLC Focus areas are not your strengths—occasionally, most people want to experience those areas, but not for a long time. Don't go out of your way to fit them into your life, because they will creep into your life whether you want them to or not.

Think of a traffic light. Your Green is your "go." Your Yellow means "proceed but with caution" (some of us are tempted to step on the gas so we can make it through a Yellow before it becomes a Red!) Reds "stop" you quickly and decisively.

A quick word on Reds is: Avoid them. Consider this scenario. You've saved for "the big" family trip to Disney World for two years. You'll be leaving in a week—flying down and staying at the Disney hotels. Then you find out the child next door has chicken pox. Keep yourself away from negative experiences as you would keep your children away from the child with chicken pox. You should do whatever you can to avoid Reds because they will often cause you frustration and headaches. To determine your Reds, choose the Focus area that represents what you dreaded doing and don't do very well (that is, if given a choice, you wouldn't want to have those experiences again).

Motherhood and GLC

Motherhood is unlike anything I've ever done before. In a "real job," responsibilities are usually well-defined and come one at a time. Before becoming a mom I worked as a quality control manager for a medical manufacturing company. My responsibilities were clear cut, I was able to finish tasks, and I got paid well for my work. As a mom I find I'm watching the children while doing dishes, watching the children while shopping, watching the children while visiting friends, watching the children while cooking, watching the children while paying bills, and watching the children while trying to spend time with my husband. I also cook while I clean. I pay bills when I watch television. Thus as a mom I do more in tandem. Motherhood is a multi-function job and difficult to dissect into segments.

Here is how I evaluate whether my activities need to be adjusted. I ask myself overall how I feel. How satisfied am I in my current lifestyle? I rate my fulfillment from one to ten, one being the least and ten being the most. If my fulfillment factor is less than five, I take steps to improve. If my fulfillment level is between 5-7, that is good. It's about average, but there is still room for improvement. If my fulfillment level ever gets above seven I'll be amazed. If your fulfillment level is above seven, then this book will help to reinforce why you are doing so well.

My Mothering Style

My Green is Ideas, my Yellow is Tasks, and Strategy and Relationships are equally Red for me. I share my Green Light Profile with you so that you can have an example of how to evaluate your fulfillment level.

Here are the activities I do every day, every week, or nearly every week:

Activity	GLC Rating
Taking care of kids	Red
Teaching kids	Green
Disciplining kids	Red
Running errands/shopping	Red
Cleaning house	Red
Cooking 3 meals a day	Red
Researching, conceptualizing, and writing	Green
Reading	Green
Finances for moms group	Yellow
Entertaining/hosting parties	Red
Fixing up my old house	Yellow
Attending church, moms	Yellow
Spending time with International Students	Yellow
Spending time with husband	Red
Spending time with friends	Red
Exercising	Red

Here's how each of my activities received its rating of either Red, Yellow, or Green. Any activity that mostly involves my primary strengths I rated Green. Those activities bring the greatest sense of satisfaction; I do my best work in those areas.

Any activity that mostly involves using my secondary strengths I rated as Yellow. I do those activities fairly well and receive some fulfillment from them. But if I do them constantly, they can turn into a Red.

Any activity not specifically in my Green Focus area (Ideas) or my Yellow Focus area (Tasks) receives a Red. When I'm doing those activities, I'm not using my greatest strengths or doing what I naturally enjoy doing. If possible, I should avoid doing Red activities for long stretches of time without a break, or at least minimize their negative effects by combining them with activities in my Yellow or Green Focus areas. Avoiding Reds altogether is impossible because many legitimate and good activities in life are Reds for somebody. The key to dealing with them is to make sure you're mixing in some Greens and Yellows.

Values

Spending time with my kids, my husband, and my friends are Reds for me. Should I avoid them because they are not in my Green Focus area? A good question. Time with family and friends is a Red for me based on my Profile, but there are also values that must be considered. I value people. It's encouraging to get together with my friends to share our lives, our joys, and our struggles. Nothing on earth compares with friendship. Friends are people who can be honest with you and fun with each other. But I am not a natural initiator and I don't need as many friends or as much time with friends as other women that I know. Values can supersede ratings of Red, Yellow, or Green; spending time with people who are important to me is one case in which they do.

Taking care of children would be a Red for me if I just took care of the kids. Relationships—spending time with people—is a Red Focus area for me. However, there are two qualifications in my Green Light Profile. The first is that I love my children and value spending time with them. The second is that I love to teach them, so I try to teach them something every day. I teach them or learn from them in order to boost an otherwise Red activity to a Yellow; that is, I try to accomplish a Green task (teaching or learning) while doing a Red (caring for kids). I do this by reading books to them, taking them to the library, to museums, to the park, and teaching them when we are outside. Usually I can tell when they've had enough teaching and then I stop.

Yellows

My Yellows are those activities that use my secondary strengths (Tasks). Handling the finances and directory for the moms group is good for me to do in small doses. Too much of those activities would make them Reds, in effect, for me. Another Yellow for me is renovating our old house and the old furniture and other items that we buy. Because I am Yellow in Tasks, this can mean renovating part of our old house that we live in—painting or wallpapering a room, refinishing an old table, or planting flowers. Because we have an old house, I've done so many of those jobs that I have pushed this Yellow into feeling like a Red for me.

Reds

My solid Reds are running errands, going shopping, cleaning, and cooking three meals a day. There is not much good for me to say about such activities. I usually cannot learn while doing them (the exception is when I learn new recipes or learn new cooking methods). I usually cannot improve doing them, because they are routine. I get some fulfillment from improving recipes, or improving my efficiency in running errands, or improving my time in cleaning my house. But usually the

Red wins out as I don't make time to improve recipes on a consistent basis, and I almost always get behind the slow driver or in the slow checkout aisle in the supermarket. My children have nearly shut down my housecleaning abilities. As I clean through one section, they are right behind me making more messes. I try to do household chores with a good attitude because I am able to squeeze in Green activities, and because they must get done. But my quality standards for them are relatively low. I'll say more about household chores in Chapter Eight.

Greens

However, activities such as researching, conceptualizing, writing, and reading give me fulfillment on a regular basis. In each of those activities I am learning, so they are solidly in my Green Focus area. I try to do them as often as possible. I am confident of my abilities when doing my Greens. When people see me doing them, they tell me I am doing a good job. I feel good about myself and this increases my self-esteem (not to the point of arrogance, for there are many activities that I cannot do well and many more that I do not enjoy).

On a periodic basis I like to include some Green activities into my schedule. As an Ideas person these would be attending a weekend conference so that I can just learn the whole weekend. Or attending a seminar on writing for an afternoon or for a couple of days or vacationing in a new place, exploring the local attractions. Staying up very late to read a good book is another example.

Green Plus Red Equals Yellow

Activities which involve doing some Reds and some Greens I rated as Yellows. Some activities, such as entertaining, attending moms program and church, and being involved with the LIFE program, are pure Yellows. Those activities would be Reds except that I squeeze learning into them. When entertaining, I learn from my guests and ask a lot of questions. At the moms program I learn a lot about the how tos of raising children—what works and doesn't work for other people. And I learn about different cultures in the LIFE program because this program is for international college students. But without learning and observing, and without valuing people, many people-intensive activities such as those would be Reds for me.

Fulfillment levels

Gets a little complicated doesn't it? It not only matters what you do but why you are doing it and how long you did it that matters. If I can squeeze in some learning throughout my day or do some tasks, such as editing or handling finances, I am a much happier camper. On days when I wasn't able to do those two things I felt a bit grumpy and out of sorts. But when it gets to be weeks and months before I really spend some extended time in my Green Focus area, I'm an awful person to be around. I get more impatient with my kids, my husband, other drivers, my friends, and myself. I feel frustrated. I feel unfulfilled. I don't like myself or my lifestyle very much. At those times I'd say my fulfillment level is about a 3 or 4.

But it pays to be realistic. Be careful not to ask, "What is my fulfillment factor today?" but, "What has my fulfillment factor been over an extended period?" You will have bad days, days or stretches of days when nothing seems to go right. Children get sick and emergencies happen. But in terms of your overall lifestyle, your goal should be to raise your fulfillment level to five or higher on a consistent basis.

Your Mothering Style

Through all of the changes that motherhood has brought, you no longer have to feel like Alice in Wonderland. You can be confident that you have unique skills, distinctive ways to plan, and concrete means to help and give to others through those skills and plans.

Maybe you're wondering what you will do now because you know your Green Light Profile. It's good to know your Greens, Yellows, and Reds, but unless you find some way to put them into practice, to use your unique skills and talents, you will not be fulfilled. In fact if you don't use your Green you may be more frustrated because now you know what makes you fulfilled. Knowledge without application often leads to frustration. But on the positive side, as Tim Kimmel writes, "Well managed talents . . . give a person a strong sense of purpose and value."[2]

So at this point your soul searching is only partially completed. You need a handle, a means, to manage your talents well. In the next chapter I'll introduce the importance of motivation in using your skills. Motivations and values combine to form *lifetime dreams*. Without a purpose and a plan, skills cannot be well-managed.

Throughout the remainder of this book I'll discuss how to manage your talents well. You'll look at the many aspects of being a person, wife, mom, and homemaker. As you examine these issues in depth, I'll give you practical tips on how to squeeze your Green into your responsibilities. You'll look further at what a Green Focus area is and how it affects your life. I'll also discuss how to handle your Yellows and your Reds. By adjusting expectations in your life around your Green Light Profile, you'll find your mothering niche, raise your fulfillment level, and chip away at the monstrous images of the Perfect Mother.

Only you can apply the Green Light Concept to your life. After all, "The challenge for us as . . . mothers is to be at peace with ourselves as we develop our own styles of mothering."[3] The women who are comfortable in their mothering niche have done this. As you continue to examine mothering in light of your Green Light Profile, remember that only you can make the changes.

The ABCs of GLC

If you want to delve a little more deeply into identifying your Green, Yellow, and Red Focus areas, this three-part chart can walk you through the steps.

A. Identify What You Do Well and Like to Do

Find the category in the chart below (Strategy, Tasks, Ideas, or Relationships) that best describes what you have enjoyed and done well. That is your Green. Which have you enjoyed most next? That is your Yellow. Circle your Green and put a box around your Yellow.

Strategy	Tasks
• directing • selling with convincing • competing • speaking	• organizing or maintaining • repairing or building • operating or controlling • troubleshooting or training
Ideas	Relationships
• researching • writing or teaching • designing • producing/performing	• visiting or building relationships • coaching or teaching • counseling or encouraging • coordinating or PR representative

Continued

B. Identify What Goes
Through Your Mind

Find the category in the chart below that best describes what goes through your mind when you're doing well and enjoy what you're doing. That is your Green. Which category describes your thoughts next best? That is your Yellow. Circle your Green and put a box around your Yellow.

Strategy	Tasks
How can I • win? • compete best? • gain people's backing?	*What can I do to* • make it better? • improve it? • keep things running smoothly?
Ideas	Relationships
I pondered how I could • get complete understanding • express it creatively • make others understand	*I thought about who* • needed encouragement • needed help • needed a listening ear

Continued

C. Identify What You Contribute

Find the category in the chart below that best describes what you contribute when you are doing what you do well and enjoy doing. That is your Green. The category that next best describes what you gave is your Yellow. Circle your Green and put a box around your Yellow.

Strategy	Tasks
I passed on • organizational growth or profits • strategies to compete and win • more adherents	*I passed on* • neatness and orderliness • correctly completed job • efficient solution
Ideas	Relationships
I passed on • new ideas and concepts • new designs • new products	*I passed on* • encouragement • personalized, unique help • concern and care

Tally the Results

Which category did you circle most often? _____
This is your Green.

Which category did you put a box around most often? _____ This is your Yellow.

Which category did you mark least or not at all? _____
This is your Red.

How Greens and Reds Make You Feel

Green:
◆ Most Effective
◆ Most Productive

Red:
◆ Less effective
◆ Less productive

By-products of Green work

A person is most apt to be...

1. Satisfied
2. Decisive
3. Positive (attitude)
4. Self-starter
5. Organized
6. Cooperative
7. Have positive relationships; Have their best people skills
8. Hopeful, excited
9. Have positive stress
10. Team player/ contributor
11. Have high energy
12. Find meaning and purpose from their work

By-products of Red work

A person is most apt to be...

1. Dissatisfied
2. Indecisive
3. Negative (attitude)
4. Procrastinator
5. Disorganized
6. Less willing, reluctant
7. Have negative relationships; Have poor people skills
8. Gloomy, down
9. Have negative stress
10. Withholder
11. Have on-again, off-again spurts of energy
12. Find little meaning or purpose from their work

© Hagstrom Consulting

Chapter 4

Dream Makers

--------◆--------

In the children's section of our local library there is an incredible book called *I Wish I Had a Big, Big Tree*. Written and illustrated by two Japanese artists, Sato and Murakami, it offers hope in the pursuit of dreams. Little Kaoru, a boy of about seven or eight years old, has a dream to own a big, big tree with a playhouse where he can make pancakes and be friends to the many birds and animals who would live in or use his tree.

First he shares his dream with his mother. She squelches him by saying, "It might be dangerous." He continues to share his dream while she looks around at their resources, which she declares are ". . . only three little bushes . . . no good at all for climbing."[1]

Meanwhile, Kaoru continues to dream of the possibilities in having a big, big tree. Fourteen pages of dream later, he wants to tell his mother more of his dream, to which she retorts, ". . . not right now, I'm busy."[2] Still not disheartened, he visualizes the dream even more.

Draw a Picture of Your Dream

Kaoru drew a picture of his tree and playhouse, his dream. You need to do the same—to think about your dream; to draw out a plan of action in your mind and on paper (not necessarily a literal drawing, but some kind of organized description). You may have a wonderful vision of what you would like to do with your life, but how does this fit in with the rest of your life? Most moms are at a loss for the specifics of how to pursue them. Remember, you do need a road map to get where you are going in life. May I suggest a GLC road map?

A GLC road map considers who you are as a person. It relies heavily on your Green Light Profile, especially your Green Focus area. But it also goes further and challenges you to consider your lifetime dreams. Before you can set and maintain realistic expectations, you need to know who you are and what your dreams are.

The What—
Defining the Dream

The *American Heritage Dictionary* defines *dream* as, "a wild fancy or hope" and, "an aspiration; ambition."[3] Cinderella, in that classic Disney film, sang, "A dream is a wish your heart makes."[4] You need to define the dream for yourself. Carl Sandburg wrote, "Nothing happens unless first a dream."[5] Therefore, the first step is to define your dream and to write it down.

What I am right now is the real me. The real me is revealed in the commitments I have made because these show more than anything else my priorities and values.

But there is more that I want. There is more that I am willing to work toward. There is more to me than just what people can see now. Indeed there is more that each woman is capable of being and doing to make a difference in this world. Potential is the capacity for growth or development; lifetime dreams can help change potential into reality.

You may feel that your dream is a mere diversion—a part-time or a pie-in-the-sky, vague hope. Don't kid yourself. Your dream is your passion, though perhaps sidelined for the moment because of your season in life. It is how you envision yourself someday.

The potential you is what you envision for yourself when you have quiet moments to yourself, when you can see past the piles of dirty dishes, the crumbs and sticky juice on the kitchen floor and the end of the day. The potential you is what you picture when you can "get your act together."

But in your situation as a mom you may ask, "Why should I dream?" Or even, "Who has time to dream?" It may seem hopeless to dream when sometimes your biggest wish is for strength just to make it through the day. On the contrary, dreaming the right dreams can encourage you in your struggles. "Hope is a waking dream," wrote Aristotle.[6] And according to the Bible, "Where there is no vision, the people perish."[7] Abandoning a dream won't literally kill you, but it may make you feel as if you'd like to die. Meanwhile, you will slowly die emotionally and spiritually. This is how I feel when I don't remember my vision or dream for the future; when all I can see around me is the cluttered house with two preschoolers and when I think of my endless "To Do" list.

It is not my intent to overwhelm you with another expectation or obligation to add to your already busy life. I am where you are right now—raising children. My kids are preschoolers, my day is full, and my lifestyle is best described as controlled chaos. But while it takes some honest soul-searching, the outcome is worth it. Beginning to develop lifetime dreams gives you a standard for evaluating your many commitments. Dreams are not meant to burden and complicate your life. Rather they, along with your Green Light Profile, help establish realistic expectations for you.

Clarifying and writing down my lifetime dream has given my life greater focus. I cannot honestly say that my life has been simplified, but it is more focused. Before, I was the woman who ran around and did everything, in effect accomplishing nothing. Now I know what I am accomplishing. My life isn't simple because I do a lot of juggling, and I am busy. But I am content and satisfied in my efforts.

Whether or not you pursue your dreams, as a mom you are probably very busy. Kaoru's mom's words, "not right now, I'm busy" are all too true of many of us. Life may pass you by if you're too busy to stop and evaluate what you want to make of it. Simultaneously enjoying the present and looking forward to the future can be difficult to do.

So begin by asking yourself:

> What is the one (or two) main goal(s) I would like to reach in life and/or make a contribution to?

Right now take a few moments to reflect on what you see yourself being and doing. What has God been whispering in your ear? What do you see beyond the dishes, the diapers, and the dailies? Take as long as you need to reflect. I don't believe in the "all you need to do is to visualize it for it to come true" philosophy. I think it's off-base to think that way because no one can promise results. However, I cannot go from New York to Boston unless I know that I want to go to Boston. So where do you want to go in your life? Knowing where you want to be will open your eyes to the opportunities so that some-day you may arrive at your destination. As Edgar Allen Poe said, "They who dream by day are cognizant of many things which escape those who dream only by night."[8]

One final note on defining your dream: For some people defining and declaring lifetime dreams is impos-sible. These people may be bright, intelligent, and cap-able. However, they have a block in the area of strategic planning. If you are one of those people, try brainstorm-ing with another person. Choose a person who knows you well. Then talk about what you like to do, who you enjoy spending time with, and what concerns you most in your life. Your friend may be able to help you pinpoint your dreams.

The Why—
Motivating Yourself

Mrs. James Brady has spent the last ten years lobby-ing and campaigning for the restricted use of handguns. It is an understatement to say that her life has not been the same since a bullet intended for President Ronald Reagan lodged itself in her husband's skull. What about Ryan White's mom being an advocate for people with AIDS? Another mom took a circumstance completely beyond her control, a circumstance that could have ruined her life, and used it to found MADD, Mothers Against Drunk Driving. Perhaps you have had such a drastic, life-altering event in your family or in your circle of close friends. If so, it may be a part of your lifetime dream.

Other people have been inspired to help those less fortunate than themselves. They have a dream to make the world a better place in which to live. Mother Teresa comes to mind. She has poured her very being into helping the poor people of Calcutta. Day in and day out she helps and gives. She is a remarkable woman who functions in the roles of Relationships and Tasks. It is beyond me where she finds the strength to serve, until I remember her God. She sees Jesus in each of the poor people she serves and because of this she continues her work.

Sometimes a dream can result from a personal failure. As an example, I think of Chuck Colson. He was imprisoned for Watergate crimes he committed during Nixon's administration. A few years after being released, he realized he had a strong desire to help others in prison, and so he founded Prison Fellowship. This desire would probably not have been revealed had he not experienced personal failure and prison life firsthand.

Perhaps you pursue your dream because you really enjoy doing the work. In the movie, *Chariots of Fire*, an actress' response to why she likes to perform on stage is simply, "I do it because I love it."[9] The Green Light Concept encourages you to do what you love doing—a good reason to base your lifetime dream on your Green Light Profile.

Maybe you've wanted to follow in your father's or mother's footsteps or accomplish something your parents never were able to do. Perhaps you've been inspired by a teacher or someone you admire. These too are valid dreams if you are not pursuing them out of guilt or pressure.

It is interesting to see where your heart's desire has come from, but sometimes the desire is just there. You cannot explain it or know where it comes from, but your dream is something that you've wanted to pursue for a long time.

Not everything can be looked at exclusively through Green lenses. Values, difficult life circumstances, and so many other variables factor into a person's dreams. As in some of the examples above, some people change for the better through disastrous circumstances. Also, character can be developed when we live responsibly with the limitations brought on by other family members—perhaps a disabled child, a permanently ill spouse, or an aging parent.

In other words, while you should look to the Green Light Concept for help, you shouldn't ignore pressing needs just because they are not in your Green. To do so would be irresponsible. Rather, your life incorporates those around you while you juggle and balance all the more to try to meet your individual needs through the pressing, urgent, and permanent needs of other family members. So you may choose to pursue a dream which is outside of your Green Light Profile because your heart has been personally touched by adverse circumstances.

Of course, not all of your life dreams have to be in your Greens. Some of mine are not. Yet I recommend basing at least one of your major life dreams on your Green Light Profile, using your Green. It gives your dream a good foundation. I like to think of GLC as the roots of a dream. It gives a form of stability because you are confident you have the abilities and the desire to continue with the dream.

Lifetime dreams not based on your strengths, apart from a strong motivation from some other source, are unlikely to come true. If your dream does not involve using your Green Focus area, you are not likely to pursue it consistently and long-term. You're not likely to have the perseverance to complete it. I love Thoreau's advice: "Do what you love."[10] The best motivation comes from doing what you love and doing what you do well.

There is another aspect to the *why* of your dream—make sure that you wholeheartedly believe in it. Your dream should be within your acceptable values. You should pursue the dream only as it is legally and morally right. Your dream and your values should be in sync, so that you can be true to yourself in pursuing your dream. But until the dream is clear to you, don't be afraid to brainstorm. Your first ideas may seem selfish, but as you think them through or talk to others, they may reveal something purposeful.

My husband and I have chosen to use the Bible as the foundation for setting dreams and goals. We have a relationship with Jesus Christ and want to serve Him. A verse from the Bible that speaks to this aspect is from the book of Philippians. It reads, "Do not merely look out for your own personal interests but also for the interests of others" (Philippians 2:4, NASB). Thus, we have a shared life dream of working in a third world country to provide technical creativity and support in developing renewable energy resources. Have we done it yet? No, but we're working toward that dream, step by step.

The key question to ask yourself for the *why* is:

> *What do I really want to do? What needs or issues stir my mind and feelings so deeply and profoundly that I want to take action?*

The Who—
Specifying a Group or Person

Another means of focusing and narrowing your lifetime dream is by deciding to help a particular person or people group. In this way your efforts are concentrated and focused. I cannot have a vision for the whole world, but I can have thoughts of working with one person or group of persons. For example, I spend time with my family, other moms, and International college students.

Not everyone has my philosophy of helping others. It is a decision I have made based on my values. Meeting just my own needs is not completely fulfilling to me. Serving only myself does not bring contentment or joy. John Mason Brown wrote, "Happiness comes from squandering ourselves for a purpose."[11] Based purely on the Green Light Concept, different people will squander themselves on different causes. The "Fruit of Our Labor" chart shows what people in each GLC category will typically spend his or her time, talent, and energies on (see pages 82 and 83).

As a mom you may feel that you are already helping all of the time. You may be asking, "She wants me to do more?" No, I want you to decide what you will do instead of saying yes to every opportunity. In this way you can meet people's needs and use skills that are unique to you. As Richard Hagstrom points out in his seminars, all responsible people have a desire to see results—fruit from their labors and satisfaction for their labors. It is good to accomplish goals and enjoy accomplishing them. If you can meet people needs too, I think that only adds to the satisfaction.

The How— Developing a Plan

How do you go about developing a plan of action for your lifetime dreams? Again I refer you to the "Fruit of Our Labor" chart. You can begin to develop a game plan by using the skills listed for your Green Light Profile, your Green Action Skills. For example, Relationships people would spend time coaching or training and building relationships.

You knew that the dreaded word *goals* would appear somewhere in this chapter. Goals may intimidate you, as they intimidate many people. I'll encourage you by adding that when you are functioning in your Greens you will be self-motivated, find meaning and purpose from your work, and be a person who often completes her goals. When functioning in your Reds the opposite will be true.

Differentiate Between a Goal and a Dream

Many times people set goals before they establish lifetime dreams and before they look at themselves. Richard Hagstrom holds that goals and plans evolve from purpose and philosophy, not vice versa. Goals in and of themselves can be fruitless and unfulfilling to a person unless a person has a real heart to accomplish them. People often make goals and plans without thinking about purpose and philosophy. Many times I said to myself, *I must set goals.* But what were those goals to be based on? I no longer make goals for the sake of making goals. Rather goals that I make are for the sake of accomplishing my lifetime dreams.

If you have a problem with the word goals, like I do, then use this definition: Goals are little steps taken to help you achieve your dream. A goal is definable and measurable. A goal only depends on me to achieve it; thus, it cannot rely on the help of other people. A goal cannot rely on circumstances or "luck" or factors beyond my control to be achieved.

However, a dream is a lot riskier than a goal. Dreams may never come to fruition, even though you have accomplished all of your goals. Dreams may depend upon circumstances, other people, and sometimes miracles. Consequently, dreams may disappoint you. But goals depend only on you. Unmet goals point the finger of blame squarely at one person, you. With unmet goals you can be rightly disappointed at yourself for lack of discipline or persistence.

I've covered the *what, why, who,* and *how* of drawing your lifetime dreams. Now it's time to move on to the arena of allowing others to know your dreams . . . which is always a little scary.

The Exposure— Share the Dream

I like little Kaoru's persistence in sharing his dream. He tried his mother a few times with no encouragement. Still that didn't stop him. Next, he shared his dream with another person, his father, who happened to have the same dream when he was a boy. I think one of the reasons we love children so much is that they are uninhibited and honest with themselves and others. And they are honest about their dreams. As adults we often lose that optimism to pursue our dreams. Realism and reality set in and we lose sight of the dream or dreams we once had. Sadly, this was true of Kaoru's dad. His dad regrets that he never pursued his own boyhood dream.

I don't share the potential me with too many people. I am afraid they will laugh because how I want to be or what I want to do is so different from how these people perceive me. Sometimes I fear that people will think that I could never have that kind of talent or perseverance to pursue my dream.

You may have your own reason for not sharing the potential you. It could be low self-esteem, lack of a vision for your life, a feeling that you may not be successful, failed attempts at pursuing a dream, feeling that you don't have the time or money to pursue your dream, or some other reason. Walt Disney's Cinderella had her own reason for not telling her dream: "It won't come true if you tell."[12]

A positive reason for sharing your dream is for encouragement. Mutual encouragement comes from finding someone with a dream similar to yours. It's great if you are able to find a whole *group* of people who have similar dreams. Then all of you can offer concrete help and advice to one another. And mutual encouragement may give you that reason you've been looking for to persevere. I know my writers' group has always encouraged me in my dream. Also, by sharing your dream, friends may be able to give you timely counsel and advice. Remember that a person of understanding and vision will best encourage you in your life dream. "A person's thoughts are like water in a deep well, but someone with insight can draw them out" (Proverbs 20:5, TEV). I hope you are able to find such a person.

The Dream Breakers

Little Kaoru's mom saw the little bushes in the yard and concluded that not much could be done. Obviously she didn't share her son's dream. She was not a woman of understanding who could help. We adults tend to look at what is obvious in evaluating dreams. George Bernard Shaw wrote of such people, "You see things; and you say, 'Why?' But I dream things that never were; and I say, 'Why not?'"[13] We need to look beyond our meager resources to pursue the dream wholeheartedly.

In my circumstances, I can feel that others do indeed have it easier than I. In my writer's group, many of the women are in their forties and fifties with grown children. I think, *Of course they have lots of time to write, since their children are out of the house. Much of my day is spent chasing little ones, amusing little ones, and picking up after little ones. When do I have time to write?*

When my Green Light Profile was analyzed a few years ago, my heart's desire was to encourage others through writing so that they would not grow weary and lose hope. Since then I've dealt with the "what ifs" of taking a part-time job so we could afford a house in the country like we've always wanted. I've struggled with writing bits and pieces of articles and books while children napped. I've let the kids spend a half hour demolishing a box of facial tissue, grateful that they remained quiet during that time so I could think and write. I've cringed a little at paying for a baby-sitter for my work time since my income is unpredictable. I've coerced my husband into baby-sitting when he wanted to do his creative work. So like you, I have struggled, sometimes a little and sometimes a lot, with the "what ifs" of following my heart's desire. Life is rarely composed of black-and-white decisions. Life is made of little everyday decisions that determine what you will do with your life.

Be honest with yourself. What is keeping you from pursuing that which you'd really like to pursue? What are your "if onlys"? Can you list the obstacles in your way? Write these down for yourself so that you can have a list for future reference. For each of these obstacles, write down as many "solutions" as you can think of. Be creative.

Lifetime dream	Obstacle	Solutions to obstacle
_____	_____	_____
	_____	_____
	_____	_____
_____	_____	_____
	_____	_____
	_____	_____

My obstacles happen to be: (1) I don't have enough free time away from the kids to pursue my dream, and (2) I think other people are more talented than I (definitely a bout of low self-esteem). I have thought, *Who would ever want to read this book?* When I let the "what ifs" take over my vision of the dream, I can be overwhelmed and think, *Why bother?* Instead, I should remember the saying: "No noble thing can be done without risks."[14]

If I were to add a third obstacle, it would be *respectability*. Following a dream passionately makes one a bit of an oddball in our culture. You can expect to be viewed as different because you will not be like everyone else. In the movie, *The NeverEnding Story*, Bastian, a young boy, is asked by the princess, "Why don't you do what you've dreamed?" Bastian replies, "I can't, I'm supposed to keep my feet on the ground."[15] Isn't that the truth? In adult life, I feel I'm supposed to keep my feet on the ground. And that's limiting in pursuing a dream.

One other reason people don't pursue their lifetime dreams, perhaps the biggest reason or the biggest "what if," is the real possibility of failing. Failing is what happens when you do not achieve your dream. Of course, this does not mean that you are a failure, only that your dream failed. You can accomplish all of your goals and still not fulfill your dream. Life is not a fairy tale and not all dreams come true, not even with perseverance and using GLC.

Which leaves us with . . .

The Risk— Not All Dreams Come True

It was Samuel Butler who wrote, "Life is drawing sufficient conclusions from insufficient premises."[16] Basically, there are no guarantees. In the pursuits of your individual dreams, you won't know in advance what life will throw your way. Many events are beyond your control, among them, hard economic times, a job layoff, death of a spouse, death of a child, windfall money, the birth of a child, and a job promotion. Both good and bad events come your way and you can't know when those events will come. And you can't know what effect those events will have on you.

If your dream doesn't come true, you can expect to be very disappointed. After all, you have poured your very being into making your dream a reality. You may experience a degree of depression; it would be a normal response. You may have feelings of anger and frustration. However, you will need to acknowledge all of your feelings, at least honestly to yourself and perhaps to a close friend or two.

A failed dream may spur you on to pursue your dream even more. In fact, some Strategy people love the resistance in overcoming seemingly impossible situations. However, most of us would probably wilt in these circumstances.

Your dream's "failure" can inspire others to pursue the dream. Instead of viewing you as a failure, these people view you as a trailblazer. Your children or someone who has admired you may pick up where you have left off. You could be the spark for someone who might do more than you ever imagined.

Before you give up on your dream, though, consider your options:

1. *Did you overlook something that needs to be done?* Get counsel from people you know and trust. Just a few days ago our family tried a local "mom and pop" type dessert shop. We looked forward to it because we like to support other people in the pursuit of their dreams and we like to eat desserts. What a disappointment—the sundaes had

imitation whipping creme on them and other ingredients were not of high quality. I wish they had a patron questionnaire to fill out.

2. *Did you give up too soon?* Sometimes a little more time commitment can yield the desired outcome. Most of us know of Thomas Edison's classic line, "Genius is one percent inspiration and ninety-nine percent perspiration."[17] Am I giving up too soon or have I not worked hard enough?

Most people are short-range planners and can get discouraged if results are not visible quickly. The only Green Light Profile which enjoys planning long-term is the Strategy person. The other Profiles prefer more short-range kinds of planning. Also, Strategy and Tasks people tend to be more detailed in their planning, whereas Relationships and Ideas people tend to work with the need at hand or the idea of the moment. Thus, many of us are not natural planners, and we need to recognize this in ourselves.

The influence of society cannot be dismissed either. We have been conditioned by sitcoms in which problems surface and resolve themselves within thirty minutes. And companies rarely plan for the long-term; the immediate profit and loss statement has become the indicator of a successful business. Not everything can be attained instantaneously, even though society tries to teach us it can.

3. *Can your dream be refined to fit better who you are?* Maybe you've decided that the Green Light Concept is not important in the pursuit of your lifetime dreams. Base at least one of your dreams on GLC, using your Green Light Profile and Green Action Skills for guidance. Be sure you have not set goals before you have established your philosophy and overall plan.

4. *Is your dream ahead of its time?* Think of the painters, scientists, writers, and other intellectual forerunners who were snubbed during their lifetimes, yet honored in following generations. The attainment of your dream may not bring the recognition you desire.

5. *Are you trying to go it alone when you don't have to?* No one says that you have to do this dream all by yourself. Sometimes in this country I think we're a bit too "rugged American individualist" for our own good. It's not only OK, it's good to be working as part of a team effort. Strategy people tend to be the initiators to form teams of people, while Relationships people enjoy working with others as part of a team. Tasks people enjoy being a contributor to a team too. Ideas people tend to prefer working alone, except when they are brainstorming with others.

It's helpful to work as part of a team for a number of reasons. Sometimes a person does not have the Green Focus area to carry out the fulfillment of a dream. And other times the goals to be accomplished are just too great to be done by just one person. So it often means working with a group of people to pursue that dream. If your skills include supervision or coordinating, this is a possibility for you. This scenario is also a possibility if you are a visionary or a motivator.

As an example of a teamwork dream, I think of John F. Kennedy. He said, "We choose to go to the moon in this decade, and to do the other things, not because they are easy but because they are hard; because that goal will serve to organize and measure the best of our energies and skills..."[18] He used his authority and motivating skills to get the team going and to keep it funded. In this role Kennedy functioned as a Strategy person. However, thousands of engineers (typically Tasks and Ideas people) performed a lot of the planning, paperwork, and calculated projections. Those people also helped design and make prototypes. And throughout it all, Relationships people helped in public relations and in resolving interpersonal problems. Indeed, getting to the moon involved a teamwork effort.

Perhaps you can join an organization that is pursuing a dream similar to yours. Find out where and how you can use your Green in pursuing your dream. Remember that the visionary, in this case John F. Kennedy, got a lot of the credit for putting the first man on the moon, but many other people contributed behind the scenes. Otherwise, this dream would not have become a reality.

6. *If this dream is in my Green, do I need more schooling or training?* Just because something is a Green for me doesn't mean I don't need more training. Writing is a Green for me, but I attend any writer's conferences that I can. For you, some solutions include going to night school, taking adult education classes while the kids are in school, attending special workshops or conferences, doing apprenticeships, and doing internships (paid or otherwise). Some people have gone so far as to work at a company in a mismatched job for a while to get a chance at a different job in that same company that would help them to fulfill their dream.

7. *Is it time to take a break?* Know when to give up on your dream, at least temporarily, for your own sanity. If you cannot handle it any more, it's time to call it quits. This threshold varies with each individual circumstance.

The big question is, "What are you passionate about enough to pursue for a lifetime? What so grabs you that you cannot shake it, cannot get it out of your head?" Whatever your answer, do it!

The Execution—
Do It

It's taken me a while to follow my own advice. Here are words I wrote in 1986 about my writing dream...

I know that God has called me, He's given me the desire, and He's given me the ability. There's only one thing left to do; as my husband so aptly says, "Do it!" That advice is what every mom needs to hear.

The What If—
for those who don't pursue their dream

The biggest "what if" can come from not pursuing your dream. In not pursuing your dream you may feel as though you've misused your talents and time, both precious commodities. I believe it is better to have tried and failed than to not have tried at all. At the end of my life I don't want the nagging "what if" of "If only I had tried to be a writer."

Does that mean you are to drop everything in your life immediately and pursue your dream? Are you to ignore the season of life you are in with young children? No! But you should start taking some steps toward the fulfillment of your dream. I like the wisdom James Dobson gives: "My advice to you is to hold onto your dreams, but take a little longer to fulfill them. Success will wait but a happy family will not. To achieve the former and lose the latter would be an empty victory, at best."[19]

A word of caution is needed here for moms who are extremely frustrated in their roles as wife, mom, and homemaker. In your circumstances these past two chapters have encouraged you and given you hope. So much so that you may be willing to make vast, sweeping changes to your present lifestyle. *Restraint!* Begin by discussing your thoughts with your husband. Get solid counsel and advice from people who know you well enough to champion small changes and frequent evaluation. While I believe change is vitally healthy and necessary, it would be, as Dobson wrote, an empty victory if you made inappropriately fast changes and left your family and old lifestyle behind.

Restraint.

Will It Come True?

What about our friend Kaoru? Did his dream come true? The book does not tell us. You will not know, perhaps until you are old and gray, whether your dream comes true. But Kaoru's story ends with, "On Sunday Kaoru and his father planted a tree. Someday it will grow to an enormous size. But right now, it is smaller than Kaoru."[20]

Maybe your efforts at making your dream come true seem insignificant in comparison to the magnitude of the dream. Take heart; that is how the fulfillment of a dream starts for most people. An old saying asserts correctly that, "A journey of a thousand miles must begin with a single step."[21] What small step or steps can you do this week to begin the pursuit of your dream? That small step is not insignificant.

How does this dream stuff fit in with your busy life, with perhaps a husband, a child or two or more, and a home to maintain? You have to evaluate each area of your life and responsibilities in light of your dream. In the next several chapters I will discuss each of those areas, how they affect you, and what adjustments might need to be made in them so you can have time to pursue your lifetime dream while meeting your obligations. Though not an easy choice, this juggling act is praised by Mary Bateson, author of *Composing a Life:*

Things are changing so fast that people are going to have to keep modifying, adjusting, compromising, revising—doing the things that women have always done to fulfill their mixed loyalties to work and family. What seems to be problems in the way women's lives are shaped turn out to be sources of "strength and creativity."[22]

Many mothers can relate to those words; they depict our lives. We have our families and our home lives intertwined in our life purpose; in our dream. Many of us have more than one dream; these dreams can be about being a mom and a wife. When I did my life goals about six years ago I wrote, "To love my husband" and "To love my children." These life dreams came from my reading of the book of Titus in the Bible. If God wanted older women to teach His values to younger women, then I wanted them for myself. For you I hope that your family fits into your life dream and that you develop strength and creativity from the maturity that this decision requires.

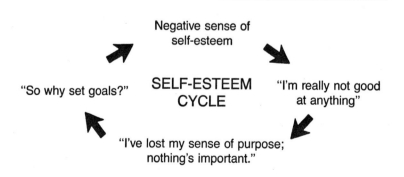

Negative sense of
self-esteem

"So why set goals?"   SELF-ESTEEM   "I'm really not good
CYCLE   at anything"

"I've lost my sense of purpose;
nothing's important."

© Hagstrom Consulting

Fruit of Our Labor

S **Strategy**	T **Tasks**
directing • profits • growth	organizing or maintaining • orderly, accurate records • neat room
selling • sales	repairing or assembling/building • runs/operates right • built right
competing • winning • top 10%	operating/handling or controlling • parts made right • accurate reports
speaking • believers • supporters	troubleshooting or instructing/training • improvements in equipment, people, or organizations
SATISFACTION	*SATISFACTION*
• *Reading organizational* *key success indicators* • *Winning over*	• *Doing every project step right* • *Straightening it out or* *making it right*

Fruit of Our Labor

I **Ideas**	R **Relationships**
researching • written report • new concept	visiting or building relationships • positive relationships • someone helped
designing • appealing design • new product	counseling or encouraging • confidence restored • someone helped
writing or teaching • book • enlightened students	coaching or training/teaching • reassure them • someone helped
producing/performing • stage play • multi-media	coordinating or PR rep/proponent • team/group effort • special occasion
SATISFACTION • *Making new discoveries* • *Producing a visible/ audible end product*	*SATISFACTION* • *Providing people-helping or special services* • *Building relationships*

GLC Profiles and Dreams

Ideas people love the possibility of dreams and like to formulate them. One of their biggest characteristics, their love of learning and ideas, can be their biggest hindrance in not concentrating or focusing on one or two important principles. And they tend not to be appreciated all of the time because their creations can be too original or offbeat for other people's sensibilities.

Tasks people unfortunately do not get a lot of credit because they often work behind the scenes. Their work tends to be very detail-oriented. They tend to think their dreams are not as big, grandiose, or encompassing as other people's, but their dreams are vitally important.

Relationships people have difficulty measuring their accomplishments. They contribute by encouraging people and helping to establish teamwork. Hence their dreams tend to elude standardized evaluation. Yet others who work closely with Relationship people often affirm and praise their important contributions.

Strategy people are the long-range, big dreamers. That's how they are designed. It's their Green Light Profile. They will be confident in their role and love the limelight that the attention brings. They need to be careful to acknowledge and thank others who have contributed to the team effort.

PART THREE

Setting Realistic Expectations in Family Relationships

Chapter 5

His Needs or Her Needs?

———————◆———————

I watched in pity. Shoulders slumped, moving at a slow pace. One deliberate step after another, as one foot lifted itself barely off the ground, skimming the sidewalk underneath slightly forward before gravity plunged it to the sidewalk pavement. I winced with each step as I peered down from my second story vantage point. One step after another, after another. I watched for a long time. I felt sorry for bodies that get old and don't work well anymore.

But as I saw this same couple time and time again my perspective changed about their circumstance. Each time I saw them walking they were together. Though their old shoulders badly slumped with the years of time and years of work, their arms interlocked one another. I began to see the ideal marriage exemplified in that older couple as they worked together to plod along.

Admiration replaced my misdiagnosis of pity. Here was a couple that exemplified what we all want for our marriages, including longevity. When I think of them it warms my heart to think of their commitment to one another. When I get to be in my eighties, I want to be walking, hand in hand, with the same man. But there's a long way from the "I do's" to the "happily ever after" of walking off into the final sunset together. If we are only in our 40s or 30s or even 20s, that's a long time until happily ever after.

Marriage is a lot of work. Just ask any couple who has made it for a lifetime. I'll never be able to forget the advice one of my aunts gave me on my wedding day. She said in no uncertain terms that she was happy for me and that there would be tough times because marriage is a lot of work. I thanked her politely and wondered why she would choose my wedding day to pass on such information. But now I know why. At the start we have ideals and hopes that somewhere along the way get altered and changed by life's circumstances. If she'd shared her thoughts at any other time it would not have made as lasting an impression as it has.

Everyone struggles at some point in their marriage. Even after seemingly perfect courtships and engagements, there are struggles in marriage. As I write this chapter, Lady Diana and Prince Charles have just had their tenth year of marriage (I hope they had a celebration). An image that remains in my mind over these ten years is their famous engagement photograph. She, wearing a casual blue shirt, hugs him from behind. Her smile is shy, proud, and happy. He's, you know, Prince Charles, but he looks extremely happy on the occasion of his engagement. The picture holds the promise and hope of engagement. Diana Spencer seems just the right kind of woman for Prince Charles. And she will benefit from his being a real life prince. Certainly theirs was a modern day Cinderella story if ever there was one. Their wedding day was magnificent; their audience numbered in the millions. They were wed; later they kissed on the balcony. Certainly here was a couple that would walk hand in hand into the final sunset.

Except that their modern day Cinderella story does not end with the carriage ride away from the wedding with the words "and they lived happily ever after." We, their audience, get a glimpse into just how hard marriage can be. We realize that no one is guaranteed a happily ever after, not even a prince and his princess. And Diana, our Cinderella, is quoted as having said, "Being a princess . . . isn't all it's cracked up to be."[1]

And while it is tragic Diana and Charles have just as hard a time of it as anyone, is it any less tragic in an "ordinary" marriage? Even though my courtship and wedding could not possibly have matched the style and grandeur of theirs, mine is nonetheless important. How do I expect to remain married if someone with such a "great beginning" as Charles and Diana have such difficulty? Still the imagination holds fast to the ideal of a permanent marriage to one man.

May I suggest that beginnings are wonderful but the least important part of marriage. My aunt was right when she said that marriage is a lot of work. Most important is the day-to-day living experiences. For while you married a man you knew, you only partially knew him. He is a package that you are unwrapping as you get to know him better by living life together. You are seeing characteristics in him that you never knew were there. And along the way he is unwrapping your package. Even what you initially liked in your package may not be appealing to you now. The same is true of you.

What to do with your package? "When you unwrap the package, you'll discover that your husband is flawed.

Aren't we all? Don't expect him to be someone he is not. Love him for who he is."[2] "All couples change. One of the unique qualities of love is its adaptability. When challenges are met with love and commitment, the result can be a strengthening of the relationship."[3]

Getting from the "I do's" to the "happily ever after"— staying married—means clearing some obstacles. By and large these obstacles are common ground for all couples. Perhaps you can list many more than the ones I'll discuss here, but I have found that the prominent ones arise from these three causes:

> My husband and I are different.
>
> My husband and I are inherently selfish in nature.
>
> My husband and I have career struggles.

But it isn't all gloom and doom. To conclude, I'll cover some encouraging aspects of marriage, relying on the words of some experts.

Differences

GLC Designs

"Why is he always _____?" You fill in the blank. What is your husband "always" doing that causes you to ask this question? Why is he always on the computer? Why is he always coaching sports? Why is he always reading? Why is he always tinkering in the basement? Why is he always working on people's cars? Why is he always talking to the neighbors or his coworkers? Why does he always want to invite people over?

If you find yourself asking those questions a lot, you have probably locked horns with your husband's GLC Profile. Your Greens against his Reds; his Greens against your Reds. At home, a person's GLC Profile shines forth.

Your husband will feel more pull to do his Green at home if his job is not well suited to him. If his job is a Red or even a Yellow, he will tend to seek out his Green after work hours. Seeing his "why is he always _____?" as your husband's Green may help you realize that your husband is not immature or selfish, but just doing what he was designed to do. If you want to know for sure, it would be best to get your husband to do a GLC Profile, then you wouldn't have to guess. If possible, have him use Appendix G.

Family Backgrounds

Sometimes husbands and wives don't realize that there were many differences in how they were brought up and in what their lifestyles were. My husband Dave and I are very opposite in family backgrounds. I'm from a large family. Our annual family Fourth of July barbecues at my grandparents' home would number in the 150 range. Dave's family considers 20 or 30 a large get-together. Dave lived in the same house all his life; I moved eight times before high school began. His parents saved for his college education; I borrowed for mine. His family goes back so far his ancestors almost came over on the Mayflower; I go back only three generations. Understandably, he relates more to the Mayflower while I identify more with Ellis Island. His parents will soon celebrate their fortieth wedding anniversary. I was twelve when my parents divorced.

Think it doesn't matter how you were brought up? Think again, because patterns of thought and response are learned early and carry on into adulthood. And marriage is something that can bring out the best and the worst in each one of us. As J. Allan Petersen wrote, "Problems in marriage will bring back the past, and the past will determine how we deal with these problems.

Your past will affect your marriage more than your marriage will alter your past. Marriage doesn't change the past; it reveals it."[4]

I think my way is right because that's how I'd do it; that's what I'm accustomed to. It helps to think that what you do is not necessarily right for other people. In many areas of life, what people say and do differently from you is nothing more than that—different. It is neither better nor worse. As Carole Mayhill wrote, "To use our differences we have to understand them, and to accept them. . . . Our differences, accepted and appreciated, are God's way of making us fit together as a couple so that we will be stronger together than either of us could be apart."[5]

However, sometimes my marriage seems more like Charles Churchill's description: "The two extremes appear like man and wife, Coupled together for the sake of strife."[6] I think that there is strife just because we are women and they are men. So GLC and understanding family differences are not enough to understand your husband fully. Even when you can look at the world through your husband's eyes—what he likes to do and does well influences his view of the world—it's not enough. The Green Light Concept provides some insights, but so does understanding basic male/female differences.

Between Men and Women

There are important differences between a man and a woman. First, a woman is made to be highly communicative. She needs time to talk alone, without the kids underfoot or as she's making supper. And she needs more than functional talk, which is talk that helps us function but doesn't bring us closer together. Here are some samples of functional talk: "Did you do the laundry? Where's my shirt? Nathan is sick. We need some more milk. The repair cost $250."

For a woman, talking isn't a nicety, it's a necessity. And we need to communicate feelings, not merely facts. Most women can handle most anything when they can really talk about it. James Dobson, Ph.D. wrote, "We human beings can survive the most difficult of circumstances if we are not forced to stand alone."[7]

Yet men and women communicate very differently. Bill Cosby agreed wholeheartedly when he wrote, "men and women belong to different species and communication between them is a science still in its infancy."[8] Recently I watched a comedian who felt that way. He wished that there was a male/female translation book, so that we could better talk to each other. Some days I'd pay almost any amount to buy one of those.

I recently found something like a male/female translation dictionary. Dr. Deborah Tannen researches the science of communication. Her book, *You Just Don't Understand*, details her research and her life struggles with communication with her ex-husband and husband. She wrote, "When sincere attempts to communicate end in stalemate, and a beloved partner seems irrational and obstinate, the different languages men and women speak can shake the foundation of our lives. Understanding the other's way of talking is a giant leap across the communication gap between women and men, and a giant step toward opening the lines of communication."[9]

Selfishness

Of course there is another reason our communication is not effective. As Larry Crabb, Ph.D. wrote, "communication problems inevitably result whenever people pursue self-centered goals."[10] One entrepreneurial couple understood this concept very well, both in their marriage and in their shared business. They wrote, "shared goals and lack of interpersonal competition are a result of their ability to communicate freely and not to put themselves above their partner or their enterprise."[11] If unselfishness is vital to a co-entrepreneurship between a husband and wife, I'd say it's vital to a marriage also.

When children come, they change the tempo of our lives, being, and marriage. Perhaps you've heard new parents refer to the days before they had kids as their "single days"; in retrospect, their added responsibilities make them feel as if they had been single when they were childless. Everyone always thinks they are busy . . . and then kids come, and wham—you feel like a two-year-old walking in front of a six-year-old on a swing. You need help.

Many new moms, instead of getting help, are at a loss as to how to communicate their feelings with their husbands, at least initially. And then when they do begin to verbalize, they often communicate ineffectively—ranting and being too emotional—causing their husbands to tune out. I quote from the book, *The Shock of Motherhood*, "Husbands don't know what their wives are going through, and they can't understand the constant exhaustion, the sour moods, the exasperations of an average day. Wives don't really know why their husbands are so dense, and that makes matters worse."[12] New moms and dads are indeed in two different worlds. Usually, his world revolves around work and her world is centered around the children.

So, with the introduction of children, marriage is not centered on romance and holding hands. Marriage is centered on deciding who's going to change the baby's diaper and who's going to get up for the middle of the night feeding. Marriage is about who is going to have a break from the kids. Although romance and feelings play a part, marriage is more about commitment, compromise, and work. It's about not being selfish when the natural tendency to be selfish is intense.

I wish all of life could be as simple as Sesame Street. I love the skits on cooperation. It's all so easy and so obvious. We learn that children shouldn't fight over a toy; they should take turns and cooperate. That's what we need to do in our marriages, except that it isn't so easy when both partners are feeling stretched and tired and taken advantage of.

Who gets the priority time and when? He's tired from a long day at work, which the commute aggravates, and he wants to do his own thing. She's been chasing toddlers, saying no, picking up spills, settling disputes, and cleaning the house that never stays clean. She's tired and she hasn't earned a cent, although she's worked hard. Who gets the priority? And who will defer? Both partners are vital and necessary to the relationship. Both have legitimate needs and desires to be met. I say again: the natural tendency to be selfish is intense.

Career Struggles

Circumstances will wear you down even when you have laid an adequate foundation. Without a good foundation of acceptance, communication, and unselfishness, circumstances can widen the gap between husband and wife. What will you do through the tough times?

There are many career situations that can really strain a marriage relationship. And these situations seem to intensify when you have children. As a woman I want to feel secure for my family, especially my children. A lot of times for me, I feel secure when my husband likes his job and his job is secure. I'll discuss some of those issues now.

Your husband may be in a profession that he loves, yet which doesn't pay well. Should you encourage him to seek a better paying position, perhaps one in management or in a new field? I cannot say. I can only say that a wife can be very influential in her husband's decision making process. Speaking from personal experience, I would rather have the headaches of balancing a tight checkbook and household, if it meant having a husband satisfied in his career, than pushing him into something he didn't like just because it paid more.

For the first few years of our marriage my husband struggled to establish his career. His first job lasted almost three years and it was never technical or challenging enough for him. Finally he started to dread it and wanted to get out badly, except no one took him seriously as an engineer. He made a jump to another job against both of our better judgments. (Desperate people do desperate things.) Now I was the one dissatisfied with his job, as he traveled most of the week. At my insistence, he left that position after one year. His next position was technical enough but the company's morale was very poor. That company closed about nine months later. It took five months for him to find a new job. He thoroughly enjoyed this job for three years, until the effects of the recession began.

Other job circumstances may force your husband to look for another job immediately or in a little while. These circumstances include a plant layoff, a company closing, quitting a job, getting fired from a job, or if your husband strongly dislikes his job. Perhaps his job responsibilities are not a match for his GLC Profile.

Whatever the reasons for his career struggles, now would be a good time for him to go through this book and to concentrate on finding a job in his Green Focus area. Support and encourage him. He will not feel good about himself as a person, which can affect how he feels as a husband and a father. Most people dislike the process of looking for a job; only a Strategy person will like looking for a job. So this situation is bad for two reasons: he has no job and it's his Red to look for a job.

Some men seem to go from career to career (job to job) or to have erratic work schedules. If that's your husband, he will need support and encouragement, but with such job chaos you will need support too. What can you do? Begin with a Green Light Profile. This Profile will help to determine if he has been mismatched to his jobs. If your husband is an Ideas person, he may get bored quickly with new jobs. Once he learns a new field and masters it, he's on to the next learning adventure. This could mean a trail of jobs behind him and before him in the future. Or it could mean that your husband needs to return to school to get training in the career that best suits him as person. Before schooling, make sure that his course of study will be concentrated in his GLC Green. Realize that during his time of schooling, money and time together will be scarce. Give him time to realize his dream and fit into a career.

I can almost hear you saying, "What about me and my needs?" You too will cause disruptions in the family with career changes, layoffs, and perhaps additional schooling. Use the same strategy as for your husband: Concentrate your time and energy on your Green and on pursuing your lifetime dream. I hope that your husband gives you freedom and latitude in your career search.

It may take time, tears, and years before your husband and you settle into a career path. And even then there are no guarantees for security in a job situation. You need to be there for each other, to encourage and help each other. And that means making the time to discuss feelings and fears. Patience is needed for a lot of tough job situations—a great deal of patience and a lot of communication. Remember that during this time you will need encouragement too. Talk with your friends about your feelings, instead of only talking with your husband. Also, you cannot be his only support; he needs a good friend too.

Realistic Expectations

I like this advice from a mom with older kids, Susan Yates, who wrote an honest book on motherhood. She wrote, "It's helpful to sit down and have a talk with one's own husband and ask him what his expectation is of me and share my feelings with him—together, as mates, we can discuss what is realistic and what isn't for our unique families. It is important that we see what is right for us."[13] An important aspect to remember is that you don't have to be like other families. You and your husband have to find out what works for you. Use the information that you have gained from your GLC Profile, settling family background differences and other sources to hammer out expectations for your marriage. Your marriage will be unique because the two of you are unique individuals. You need to develop a working relationship despite your differences.

It's not either his needs or her needs that are the most important in marriage; sometimes her needs take priority and sometimes his do. And because you have children, sometimes *their* needs take priority. From day to day and with changing projects and deadlines, I encourage you to take the time to talk with your husband and prioritize needs together. If a week goes by without having good communication time with my husband, I begin to feel frustrated. Unless a foundation for communication and understanding is established, frustration and misunderstanding will result.

The other areas of our life flow more smoothly when the husband-wife relationship is firmly established. I put the marriage chapter before the other areas of your life because I believe that your marriage is your top priority. If this top priority is being worked on and established, teamwork results. A team functions best when each partner realizes that he or she cannot do everything alone. That is the premise behind the Green Light Concept. Charles Churchill agrees with this: "By different methods men excel; But where is he who can do all things well?"[14]

An important element in your relationship will be the lifetime dreams that each of you has personally and both of you have as a couple. We discussed the concept of dreams in Chapter Four. Each partner needs time to pursue his or her dream. Sometimes individual dreams can seem very opposite and it may be hard for each dream to be pursued. But, "Love does not consist in gazing at each other but in looking outward together in the same direction."[15] Try to share your lifetime dream with your husband, and let him tell you his. Ask each other, "What do we really want to accomplish with our lives?" Set aside a time to talk and listen and accept each other. Perhaps a weekend away can be arranged or an afternoon can be set aside for this purpose.

If your husband will not set aside time to discuss dreams and goals with you, or if dreams and goals intimidate him, I suggest bringing up the subject during travel time in the car. As a family we spend lots of time in our car for day trips and for traveling 100 miles to visit Dave's parents. We have some of our best talks on these road trips. You can avoid the words "dreams" and "goals" by first relating thoughts about what you'd like to do in the coming years, and then asking your husband what he'd like to do.

More than This

Bill Cosby's dedication in his book *Love and Marriage* says it all: "For Camille forever."[16] What a fortunate wife. When couples exchange vows most make a forever promise. Chuck Swindoll wrote, "A promise made, a promise witnessed, a promise heard, remembered, and trusted—this is the groundwork of marriage. Not emotions. No not even love. . . . Rather, a promise, a vow, makes the marriage."[17] The promise is most important to remember. And I like the definition of love from Anna Louise de Stael, because it embraces the thought of a permanent vow. Love is "a symbol of eternity. It wipes out all sense of time, destroying all memory of a beginning and all fear of an end."[18] Two weeks ago Dave and I attended the most beautiful wedding I've ever been to. During part of the ceremony the minister described the circles of the wedding rings as never ending, like the love of two married people.

Another gem from Cosby's book is his description after a fight with his wife. Right after he said to her, "Well, I just want to say one more thing that happens to be right: I love you."

"See? If you talk long enough, you finally make sense. And I love you,"[19] says his wife. God tells us of the importance of love, "Above all keep fervent in your love for one another, because love covers a multitude of sins" (1 Peter 4:8, NASB). Certainly love covers the discouragements of marriage that come from differences, selfishness, and career struggles.

Maybe you've forgotten how much you love each other with the busy first years of parenthood. It's a common problem; there isn't enough time and energy and focused attention for each other with the children demanding and needing so much time, care, and attention during the early years. It seems so obvious, but you have to make time for your marriage. I agree with the statement, "There must be something somewhere that we cannot love too much."[20] I can't remember a time when at the end of a day I thought that I loved my husband too much. Love is a debt of privilege that can never be fully paid.

How can there be time for just fun when you are so busy already with his job, your job, kids, house, family activities, and community involvement? Your busyness is precisely why you and your husband need time alone. *Time alone gives you time to rediscover each other, time to recover from the harsh blows of life, and time to renew your strengths.* In the years of being a parent of a young child, the marriage relationship often takes a back seat or gets ignored. This is most unfortunate for a marriage. Without shared time a marriage tends to die. "Again and again, I have seen that when couples put their marriage first, their children and their work fare much better; but when the relationship occupies any other place on the scale, everything else suffers. So, give your marriage the attention that it deserves. Find out each day how your partner is feeling. Take vacations without the children, spend money on yourselves."[21]

Dave and I have established a weekly date night (yes, date night) so that I can talk to him about the important areas of life without interruption. During this time I talk about feelings; I try to avoid functional talk. Occasionally, we go on a mini vacation without the kids. We leave Saturday morning, sleep at a bed and breakfast, and return sometime Sunday.

Certainly you can spend a little money on your marriage. Add up all the money you have spent on the extras for your children—preschool, dance lessons, fast food restaurants, and extra toys. Your marriage is your priority relationship and you can squeeze some money from somewhere.

Here's how Dave and I keep the cost down for our date nights. We eat out on a weeknight and order a dinner special which is usually under $7 per person. We order egg rolls and lo mein and typically our total cost is $12. We pack a picnic dinner and eat at a local park or cook a gourmet meal at home, served on the good china, and served without the kids around. Dates need not be expensive. I define a date night as an agreed upon activity where the kids are not present and there is ample opportunity and atmosphere to communicate.

Sharing time with my husband has been a significant part of our self-imposed therapy as a couple. As we have spent more time together and time away from the kids, we have rediscovered the fun of being with each other. We laugh, we talk, and it is good. I think my husband and I could claim the quote: "We took life too seriously and forgot that being playful, joyful, and laughing at ourselves, even daring to be silly, can be a most important part of life."[22]

Yet there is an inherent challenge in finding fun things to do together. Remember all the differences I discussed earlier? In my life, here's what happens. . . . I light the candles for a romantic candlelight dinner. He says, "Can I turn on the lights so I can see what I'm eating?" We wander around the video store for an hour looking at thousands of movies because we cannot agree on which one to rent; I want a video that emphasizes the relationships between people, while he wants one which emphasizes the relationships between warring nations. We compromise and neither of us is satisfied. We watch fifteen minutes or so of the movie and then resort to watching a rerun of Bob Newhart and the first few minutes of news. Then we fall asleep.

It seems that many women want romantic touches

that most husbands aren't attuned to—the kind of romance personified in the candlelit dinner, soft background music playing as you gaze intently into each other's eyes and talk and talk. Husbands who will have a naturally easier time with this kind of romance are some Strategy types (until he caught you as his prize), some Ideas men (being creative in setting the romance mood), and many Relationships men (that is their forte, spending time with people listening and meeting people needs.)

Some men go overboard in their romancing! Not mine, of course—though he's learned the importance of flowers. Some men whose Green is Relationships do a wonderful job. They naturally do things that are unique and distinctive. If you have a husband whose Green is Relationships, you may have trouble meeting his need for romance and specialness.

A Tasks man will do a good job at consistently setting aside time with you if he makes it a goal for the marriage. He will not usually be as good at setting the mood for a romantic dinner or a weekend or having fun spending time with you. He will probably need to learn to loosen up and have fun for your sake. But based on his Green, he won't loosen up much. Some men in this style will never see the need for spending the time or money on a bit of romance. It can be like romancing the stone.

Happily Ever After?

What GLC Profiles fit best together in marriage? And which are the most likely to have a happily ever after marriage? Those are deceptive questions. The best marriage does not depend upon putting this GLC Profile with that GLC Profile, but upon acceptance of each other and commitment to each other. Yes, there are a few people who naturally seem to dovetail in their needs and

It's best to respond to our husbands maturely—loving, valuing, and accepting them. However, we don't always respond as we should. Rather, our thoughts and words tend to be reactions instead of responses. The chart below lists ways wives react to their husbands. Find your GLC profile and your husband's GLC profile and where they intersect. This intersection shows how you'll tend to react to your husband.

		Wife's GLC Profile			
		S	**T**	**I**	**R**
Husband's GLC Profile	**S**	• We're too much alike • We compete fiercely about everything • Neither of us feels like doing the routine, detail work	• He never handles the details properly; usually he doesn't handle them at all • He's always talking about ten years from now; what about today and next week? • He's always in such a rush	• He's always on a deadline; I wish he could take time to smell the roses • I hate when he speaks off the cuff without researching the facts • He's such a salesman that he embellishes the facts	• He's always going, going, going, doing, doing, doing; I'd like a slower pace of living • He doesn't take into account my feelings; he bowls me over • He never wants to spend time with our friends
	T	• He analyzes everything to death • He should learn how to speed things up; not everything has to be done perfectly. • He's too focused on the details	• We're too much alike • We drive each other and our friends crazy because everything has to be "just so" • We get caught up in the details and can't see the big picture	• He does everything by the book; he's not creative at all • Everything is always "detail, detail, detail"; I wish he would free flow think sometimes • He always does everything the right way; he's not much fun	• He's always concerned about facts and details; people don't seem important to him • He always complains about the house being messy; he expects me to be the perfect cleaner • What I do never seems good enough for him

Wife's GLC Profile (cont.)

		S	T	I	R
Husband's GLC Profile (cont.)	**I**	• He's so vague about when something will be completed • He always wants to learn and know more, but he doesn't accomplish anything • Why can't he do something else besides writing and painting?	• He can't finish anything because he keeps starting new projects • He has clutter, books, and paper everywhere; it drives me crazy • He should budget his time and money better	• We're too much alike • We're always trying something new, struggling to find time for our ideas • We feel like we are in separate worlds sometimes	• He's always researching and analyzing things to death • He'd rather be inventing a new product than eating dinner with us • Our basement looks like a chemistry lab
	R	• He's too sensitive and emotional • He lets people take advantage of him; I wish he would stand up for himself • He'd do anything for people without regard for himself	• He's with people all the time; he doesn't have time to handle our finances • He's a bleeding heart; I don't see why he's so emotional • I wish he wouldn't have people over all the time; I like quiet in my house	• He spends too much time with people • I can't believe he doesn't read more • He doesn't appreciate fine arts and the theater	• We're too much alike • We have people over all the time • We often ask, "Who's going to pay the bills and clean the house?"

desires. But there is no one combination of people who have the best marriage. Rather, happily ever after marriages come as partners work together and accept one another's uniquenesses, family backgrounds, and gender differences. They make ways for each of them to pursue their dreams, supporting each other through whatever life brings their way. Somehow they make time to enjoy each other. They allow each other to grow and develop as people. They give each other tender loving care because they choose to love each other unselfishly.

The worst case scenario is where there is no understanding of one another. This relationship could be described as, "two are walking apart forever, and wave their hands for a mute farewell."[23] And with a divorce rate of nearly 50 percent, many couples are indeed walking apart, even though they are married. Divorce is the final farewell between two people that have been walking apart for some time.

Remember that old, slowly walking couple at the beginning of this chapter? I want my marriage to last like that. As James Dobson, Ph.D. wrote, "What do women most want from their husbands? . . . the assurance that 'hand and hand we'll face the best and worst that life has to offer—together.'"[24]

Chapter 6

Every Child a Surprise

———◆———

I panic as I hear a gagging noise from my son Nathan's highchair. Immediately I think, *He must be choking.* I look. Instead he is vomiting. I am relieved to know that he is not choking on food that I didn't cut quite small enough. But now I am worried that he is sick. *Not again. Oh, he can't be sick again.* More of his food comes up. *Yes, he's sick.* It's spring in New England but this past winter was terrible. With widely fluctuating temperatures I had many sleepless nights and I felt I singlehandedly paid for my pediatrician's vacation. Then suddenly Nathan seems OK. Now he is almost laughing. *Just a minute, hey wait, you did that on purpose.* I say to my husband, "He did that on purpose." Separately my son eats many of these ingredients. He loves scrambled eggs and cream; he eats cheese on fast food establishment cheeseburgers. Yet combined in the form of quiche, it is intolerable to him.

My husband smirks, "It's true, real little boys don't eat quiche." I am not amused. How could he do that? I'm still not sure. I am surprised.

One certainty I love is that every child is a surprise to most marriages, not for being unplanned but for the way he or she changes your life. Until you're a parent you don't really know what "on call 24 hours a day" means. And even though you've read the books and talked to friends who have children, it's impossible to describe the surprises that children bring.

Many mothers feel a need for a break from the children. After all, unlike taxi drivers, you can never put on your off-duty sign. Kids are demanding and have their own minds and want their own way, not your way. By a certain time of day you certainly do need a break from the kids. My break time usually happens around 2:00 P.M. By that time I am supersaturated with being around kids. I understand fully why, too. After all, "Youngsters between two and five years of age have an uncanny ability to unravel an adult nervous system. Maybe it is listening to the constant diarrhea of words that wears Mom down to utter exhaustion."[1]

However, moms need a break not only to escape the constant demands of children, but also to do something Green. Again, I look at my GLC Profile. Of the activities that I enjoyed doing and that I did well, none involves doing them with other people. Primarily, I like to do things by myself. So, where does motherhood fit in when my kids are near me, tugging at me and talking to me most of the day?

How to Get Time Away from the Kids

Here are some strategies that I've used effectively. Not all methods will work for you. When you use these strategies, remember to do an activity based on your GLC Profile, preferably in your Green Focus area. Don't do housework unless housework is your Green. (Yes, some people's Green involves housework.) Use this time to rejuvenate yourself by concentrating on your Greens.

Nap Time

Take advantage of your children's sleeping to do activities in your Green Focus area. Don't do house-cleaning unless it is a Green for you or unless it is an unusually high priority that day.

Quiet Time

This is useful if your child has outgrown naps or never napped in the first place. At a certain time of day she is to remain in her room for a half hour to an hour. Explain to your child that she is not being punished. I often say I'm fussy or I'm tired, and I let my daughter know verbally that I am not mad at her but that I need some alone time. First start with small increments of quiet time. Begin with five or ten minutes and gradually build up to a half hour or an hour.

Video Time

I usually don't put on a video until I'm tired. This relieves some of the "guilt" I feel for putting my child in front of the television. Also, I usually put the television on the public channel, so when the tape stops, "Sesame Street," "Mister Roger's Neighborhood," or some other educational show automatically comes on. I rely on videos, as other moms do, when I have previewed the show that is on and have approved it for my child's viewing.

Wait Till Dad Gets Home

My friend's husband watches their child every Monday night so that she can concentrate on sewing and making things with her hands. Another friend of mine has three boys, and when dad gets home the boys gravitate toward him. By this time of day she enjoys not having the children with her and has some free time.

Swap Kids

Take turns with a neighbor once or twice a week and trade off kids. Spend the time pursuing your Green.

Hire a Baby-sitter

Arrange for a sitter (perhaps someone in junior high or senior high) to watch your kids for an hour or more. With the availability of part-time jobs to high schoolers, it's a good idea to set a weekly schedule with your sitter for a specific day of the week and for a specific time.

Co-ops for Baby-sitting

I've not known them to work that well, but it's worth a try. If it works, you'll be saving a sizable chunk of money. The best option available is to occasionally swap child care with a friend.

Mini Breaks

These strategies are not enough to do a big project but may give you some time to think and clear your head, perhaps even get a good idea or two.

Change of environment. Take the kids out for a walk in the stroller. Stop at a doughnut shop and buy a few doughnut holes or another special treat.

Change of pace. Sometimes just a change of routine will be enough of a break. I put the kids in the bathtub with some fun things to play. The water changes their moodiness.

Different settings. Make a tent for the kids to play in inside of the house. Tell them they must play quietly with their friends (stuffed animals and dolls). Or let them have a table so that they can set up a tea party for their friends and serve water and graham crackers.

You may be thinking, *I'd never manipulate my children like that just to get a few minutes or hours of peace and quiet.* I think that the old Perfect Mother tape plays for a lot of us . . . "a good mother wouldn't do that." But a sane mother does, and with relatively little guilt, for several reasons. There will always be some guilt; after all you are a mother. But it doesn't mean there always should be. I don't feel guilty for getting time away from my children because I take good care of them. And I take good care of them partly because I use these techniques to recharge my emotional and mental batteries. If I'm not recharged, then I'm not a very good mom to be around. So when I'm with them, I try to be really with them. I spend quantity and quality time with my children—by listening to them, learning about them, loving them, and at times changing my plans to meet their needs and sometimes their wants. I don't want you to feel guilty about some much deserved time away from your kids, because the bottom line is that they benefit from it too.

But I also squeeze in some of my Greens even while I'm with my kids. . . .

How to Go with Your Greens

You've got to find some Greens in your responsibilities to your children. Yes, you'll still do plenty of tasks that you don't like, your Reds. But for the sake of emphasis, I repeat: you must squeeze in some Greens when you can.

I'm an Ideas Green and a Tasks Yellow. To squeeze in my Greens, I take my kids to places where we can learn together. The obvious places are the library and the science museum. We go to any place that animals are penned up for us to look at and observe. We go to new places and try new activities because I like to learn. And I get them involved and excited by saying, "Today we're going on an adventure!"

We also take nature walks. Because my kids are pre-schoolers, oftentimes this amounts to going around our neighborhood and observing birds and bugs. We stop and take the time to examine objects close up. We tear some leaves apart. When we get home we look up what we saw in our guide books. Lately we've even brought some caterpillars into our house so that we could watch them spin a cocoon. A few weeks later we had the excitement of seeing a new moth.

With some GLC Profiles, doing activities with your kids will be more enjoyable for you. Relationships people will enjoy being with their children most because they enjoy being with people and serving people. Ideas people and some Tasks people are good at teaching, so they will excel in that aspect of raising children. However, you need to evaluate how your child is doing with your form of motivation and whether you need to back off at times. If you're an Ideas person there are some activities that you will be able to do with your children and enjoy, especially if one of your skills is teaching, but if you are trying to make a quilt the presence of children most likely will be a problem. Tasks people generally do not like to work with people. They may have the most difficult time of all doing their Greens with their children. Strategy people do not enjoy just spending time with their children; they want to be accomplishing something else in the process.

Here are some suggestions about what you can do with your children to match your GLC Profile:

Strategy Person

♦ Be a coach for your child's team

♦ Show them how to start a small business (perhaps a lemonade stand) and do it with them

♦ Teach them about scheduling and time management principles

♦ Set goals with them and help them to follow through

Tasks Person

♦ Refinish or fix something (but not your kids)

♦ Show them how to do improvement projects, teaching them how to properly use tools

♦ Teach them how to use a computer

♦ Establish a budget with them, showing them how to save for what they want to buy

Ideas Person

♦ Sew clothes for her doll/decorate a doll house

♦ Make and paint blocks, model airplanes and tree forts

♦ Bring kids to the library and museums

♦ Visit nature centers and historical sites to do some teaching

Relationships Person

♦ Visit elderly or shut-ins

◆ Buy cookies for neighbors and make an appointment to visit

◆ Invite the neighborhood kids over for playtimes

◆ Take kids with you shopping or to parties or out to eat

◆ Just about anything you do with your children!

Children are great learners, so you can teach them about manners, values, or anything that you would like them to know more about. My background is in engineering, so I explain to my children why events happen and what makes machines work. One day I tried to explain to Hannah why an inflated balloon goes all over the place when released. I told her, "Hannah, air pushes the balloon. There's a saying that for every action there is an equal but opposite reaction." Hannah said proudly, "For every action there is an eagle action!" And this is how Newton's First Law will probably stick in her mind. I shouldn't take myself so seriously.

Child's-eye View

I have learned to see life through Hannah's eyes. Kids do say the darndest things, as an old television show quipped. And they also do the darndest things. It's such a stress reliever when I pause for a few seconds, see the situation from my child's viewpoint, and then make my response. My response tends to be laughter or shock. Laughter does not solve major problems, nor does it change situations, but it does change me and how I respond to my children. And as a mom, that goes a long way.

Emphasizing Your Child's Greens

One of the privileges of having children is being able to help them find out how they are made. It's also one of a parent's biggest responsibilities. One of the values I've taken from the Bible and made part of my life is, "Train up a child in the way he should go."[2] Sometimes this is called a child's natural bent or his special talent or his gift. It is very much like the GLC Discovery Guide in Appendix G, with the exception that your child is too young to take this type of test. She's had too few experiences. The Discovery Guide should not be administered until your child is about fifteen years old. But what are you, as a parent, to do in the meantime to help your child?

Think of your job as exposing your children to life and its opportunities. Don't protect them from exposure to preferences different from yours. You are doing this to help your children figure out who they are. Accept and encourage their design; build up their esteem. As a mom you know how great it is when you are doing something in your Green; it gives you confidence. In a similar way you want your children to be built up and encouraged. Richard Hagstrom once wrote, "Enabling coaches try to link up goals to capabilities and values."[3] Even now I'm looking at my children. I wonder what they will become as they grow up. I'm attuned to their tendencies. I give them opportunities to try new activities—such as dance class, art projects, and singing. And so do you.

But performance and levels of achievement are not my goals for young children. Rather, I want them to feel free to try out new skills and new experiences. Thus, I need to verbalize to them, "You like playing basketball," rather than, "You're a good basketball player."

Most parents have access to a number of ways to

expose children to life and its experiences. The simplest and most obvious is for you and your husband to train them at home through everyday circumstances or through planned training times. Another avenue is through schools or classes; we've taken advantage of preschool, dance lessons, Sunday school, and gym classes. Though these more formal options may come at a cost or fee, good classes are worth it. As a family you could also plan special field trips or day trips around where you live. Once a year during a part of your family vacation, you may choose to expose your children to a place farther away (we plan to visit Washington, D.C. in the next few years). As the parent, it is your choice. But use ways to expose them to what they enjoy doing and seem to do well.

As your children get older, I suggest pinpointing their Green Light Profile. Encourage them to get training, particularly if it is college (which is expensive), in their Green Focus area. Concentrated schooling in their Green is of the most benefit. After all, that's what they do best and enjoy doing the most. Such training will be a wise investment.

Projection

To project means, "To cause (an image) to appear upon a surface," and, "To form a plan or intention for."[4] As a parent it is easy for me to project for my children either through an image or a plan. An image could be something I have formed in my mind of what the "perfect child" should be or do or something tangible, such as another child or a sibling. As for developing a plan for their children, many parents do this and few admit it. Developing a plan includes wanting your children to pursue a certain profession.

Projection is expecting someone I know to be like me, to do the things that I like and to do those things well. In effect, projection rejects a person's design by deciding what that person should do and how she should do it. For example, I catch myself thinking that researching and writing is easy and that everyone should be able to do it. I forget that it's not easy for everyone. For me it's a natural strength; for other people it's a struggle. Contrarily, my Strategy friends say, "Planning ahead for one year is easy. Everyone should do it." I think, I could never do it. What I mean is that it would not be enjoyable and it wouldn't be something I'd do consistently without coercion.

Comparing Children to Others

I couldn't figure out how it happened to us. The two children we have are extremely opposite in their likes, dislikes, and temperaments. One loves to play alone, as well as with other kids, and thrives on a regular routine. The other one loves the continual company of other people and the routine of nonroutine. In my attempts to meet both of their varying needs I feel pulled in two opposite directions.

When Hannah was born she came out like a Hannah. She didn't cry loudly but came out with a coo, like the sound a dove makes. Hannah means "full of grace." And ever since she's been a bundle of pink. At the age of four she wears exclusively dresses and skirts, mainly in pinks, light blues, whites and purples. Her world is full of dolls, dress-up, tea parties, chats with other four-year-olds, dance class, and rehearsing weddings. Conditioning you say? No, I say. She does not imitate me. I'm likely to wear a dress once a week. As a girl I didn't play dress-up and dance but kick ball and foot races. I majored in engineering. This woman takes no credit for conditioning.

Enter Nathan almost three years later, all boy. After "Maaaaaa" and "Daaaaaa," his first words were "b" words: ball, bop, and bug. His world nearly two years later revolves around balls, hitting things, food, throwing things, and spotting airplanes. He's an air traffic controller assistant as he shouts, "Ook, pane" (translation: Look, plane!), whenever he hears a plane. Nathan is all boy despite an older sister who wants him to endure dress-up and tea parties.

As such, it would be easy, almost natural, for me to make off-the-cuff remarks to Nathan such as, "Hannah does beautiful art work. Why don't you try?" Or I could say to Hannah, "Nathan is such a good, quiet boy who plays by himself in his room." I could use comparison to try to change her behavior or to get her to do what I want. But I don't want my child to do emotional gymnastics for my sake. I'd rather let her be her own person, with her own strengths and weaknesses.

What do I make of the differences between my two kids? Children are not born a blank slate. When we get them they already have quite a bit of personality in them. And it is our responsibility to work within their design, which means accepting them as they are. And that means channeling energy, directing activities, teaching, and caring for them, all the while accepting our children's design and our children's personality.

Career Values and Judgments

When they dream of their children's future, many parents tend to think of professions like medicine, law, and other professional, well-paying, white-collar jobs where they can advance and have the admiration of their peers. It is better to look at their career goals based on their GLC Profile and their desires. What is best for them? How can you encourage your children based on their Greens?

My husband and I are both engineers; getting good grades was relatively easy for us. What will we do if (or when) one or both of our children does not perform as we expect them to in school? We are trying not to have unrealistically high standards for our children in the area of school grades. I'm sure you have areas in which you want your children to excel. Perhaps you even want your children to take over the family business or to pursue your career. Look at each child with sensitivity to his or her own uniqueness and not what you expect or want that child to be.

Consequences of Projection

It's easy to think that someday you'll have to be careful about projection on your children. However, you need to be concerned now, so that you don't crush their spirits. You want your children to know that you accept them without reservation and condition. Projection may appear harmless, but repeated rejection of a child's design is not wise.

Rejecting a child's design is to reject and devalue that child. That only encourages the child to change to fit an image or a plan that doesn't match how God made him or her.

Larry Crabb, Ph.D., psychologist, wrote that, "Most of us, when we look within, can put our finger on a strong desire to love and be loved, to accept and be accepted."[5] With projection the child does not experience complete love and acceptance. Sadly, with all forms of projection the parent-child relationship suffers. And so does the esteem of the child. As parents we want the best for our children, so we feel it is our responsibility to guide and offer them advice. We need to look at the advice we give with the child's design in mind.

Therefore, base your advice solidly on the Green

Light Concept. Take into consideration each child's unique design. Otherwise your children will all sense that your love is conditional. Not accepting and valuing their design will lower esteem and self confidence. They'll doubt their own strengths. Your job as a parent is to help your children go in the way that they should each go, not in the way you'd like them to go.

Focused Time with Each Child

Focused time with each child helps me avoid projection and comparison. I can see and experience what each is talented in, what each excels at, and what each loves to do. Then I appreciate each child as a unique gift. As I spend time with each child, I appreciate his and her individual strengths, personality, and temperament.

For some parents lots of individual time will be harder to come by. Those who work for pay full-time may be especially stretched. Moms with many children may find it more difficult to spend quality and quantity time with their children individually. Single moms may have difficulty making time for each child. However, it takes time and availability to make special memories and to make everyday days memorable. But it is worth it and it's part of the reason that my husband and I had children—so that we could enjoy them and spend time with them.

A Child's Audience

So far I've talked about developing just the natural skills of your child without regard for his or her character development. Your children will learn a lot from you and your values. Though I want my children to be bright, I also want them to be kind and respectful of people. Dr. Brazelton explains,

There is a kind of vacuum in cultural values for young parents. Cognitive performance is easy to measure and to demonstrate to your friends. It becomes a way for young parents to feel successful in their parenting.... Emotional development is the base for future cognitive success. An emotionally fulfilled child will also have enough self-image to care about others and be ready to give to others as well as to acquire for himself. Our society may need a serious reevaluation—we are raising children to be highly individualistic, intellectually clever, and self-motivated—to the exclusion of caring about others around them. Do we want to create cognitive monsters? or well-adjusted children?[6]

We need to applaud for children without regard to their performance, praising the children themselves and not just their accomplishments. How sad to think that sometimes a child feels more loved for what he does than who he is. I've made it my job to clap for my children and encourage them in their character development. If no one else in our competitive society will clap for them, at least my husband and I will. I hope you do the same for your kids. I like what one writer wrote, "They need an audience so much. Let me applaud them with my heart as well as my hands."[7] Kids will know if you are genuine in your approval of them—not only in your outward actions but deep down inside.

Here's how I've been applauding for my little girl in a unique way. Every once in a while I like to tell Hannah these words; it lets her know that I accept her because she is herself. I say to her, "Hannah, I'm so glad God put you in our family. You're the one for us, not Kaitlyn or Jessica or Emma. They're nice, but you're special to us." Then we give each other a knowing look and a hug. But lately she's added these words after mine, "I just want you for a mother—not Emma's mother, not Jessica's mother, not Ashlie's mother. You're the best mother." Oh gush—I just love the job of motherhood at times like that!

Relationships moms will excel in giving their children encouragement, applause, and love without regard for performance. Strategy moms tend to tie their applause with the performance of their children. Tasks and Ideas moms are not prone to those extremes; they tend to do both.

Discipline

Why discipline? As one mom wrote, "Even cute kids can do ugly things."[8] My kids are adorable—no really, they get stopped in supermarkets and blessed for being so cute, through no effort of their own. Yet they do ugly things. Thus the need for discipline. Norman Wright, a counselor, wrote, "When our children make wrong choices or misbehave, of course they need to be corrected."[9] The ultimate reason for discipline is to teach your children self-control.

Unfortunately the word discipline connotes spanking exclusively to some people. Ways to discipline differ with children and with parents. Discipline is using reasonable methods to help your children by correcting their inappropriate behavior and by reinforcing their positive behaviors and actions. My children are normal children, although at times they are strong-willed. Mostly, I use the word "no" when they are in danger. A lot of times they get sent to their room or to what I call the "whining chair" for a few minutes. Also, I've taken away privileges such as watching television or a movie or having dessert. A spanking is reserved for repeated offenses, when the above does not work and when they are openly defiant. Bill Cosby wrote about spanking a child, "We had tried all the civilized ways to redirect him, but he kept feeling he could wait us out and get away with anything. And we loved him too much to let him go on thinking that."[10]

Another aspect of discipline is encouraging correct behavior and positive character qualities. You can be your child's audience, as I described above. Use this positive and encouraging aspect of discipline. As a primary means of discipline I praise my children for what I feel are admirable qualities. If my daughter shares her cookie with her brother without being told to do so, then I tell her, "It was kind of you to share with your brother Nathan." Or if my kids have played together quietly and cooperatively for a length of time in the morning, I encourage their behavior by saying, "You guys did such a good job playing with each other this morning that Mommy had time to do all of her work. Let's go play at the park and have a picnic lunch." It may not be easy at first, but if you try you will find something to encourage your kids for. Catch your children doing something right and tell them.

When disciplining, be consistent and fair. A mom soon learns that siblings have a fierce sense of justice. They are able to discern a millimeter difference in their half of the piece of cake. One of my four-year-old daughter's favorite sayings is, "That's not fair." She says it with emphasis, and I wish you could see the look of injustice in her face that goes with it. I hear this phrase when we have an appointment and we are leaving the playground, "That's not fair. How come these other kids get to stay?" I hear it when she has to go to bed. I hear it when she thinks Nathan got better treatment than she did. My youngest is not old enough to express himself with words, but he communicates his sense of injustice clearly. When I give my daughter a cookie first, he looks at the cookie. Then he looks at her, looks at me, reaches his hand out to grab the cookie and looks at me. Then he whines while glaring at the cookie and me. But what else would you expect from kids?

The best example of firm, loving, and consistent discipline came up in one of my mothers' group discussions. The analogy goes like this. When your child is young you are like a protective fence to her. If you allow her to go through you or move you, she may be in potential or real danger, such as being hit by a car. It's your child's job to test that fence. She thinks, Is this fence for real? *Or is this fence just for show?* She wonders if this fence will protect her and help her: *Is this fence looking out for my best?* Children will test and test and retest the fence. And you are that fence. They will want to know if the fence ever moves and, if so, what kind of pressure makes it move. What makes you move? When and under what circumstances? Tiredness, fatigue, PMS, whining, having a bad day, and continual activity make me and my fence move.

How does this relate to a mother's GLC Profile? Just as we are all different in other areas, we are all different in the area of discipline too. The Relationships mom will tend to be more lenient and understanding of children's behavior. Her fence will tend to have more holes in it and will bend more, or even move. But her children will rarely doubt that she loves them.

Strategy moms may tend to be overly rigid and strict in their disciplining—the rules have been laid out and are clear in their minds. They measure behavior against goals. Sometimes their children will doubt that they are loved because Strategy moms can be so rigid. But they will value, in time, this consistency and fairness.

Tasks moms will be methodical and precise in their disciplining. They will tend to establish a system and follow it (though it will take them a while to figure out the system). People skills are not their best, so it may be hard for them to discipline. But they will tend to be fair and consistent. Children will feel secure but will tend to question Mom's love for them.

Ideas moms will envision the ideal of how disciplining should be done, then try to attain it. They will read books and do research and learn a lot about the notion. Yet they will tend to be unsure that they are doing the right thing. Their children are not sure if or when the rules will change (with moodiness or after having read a new book on discipline), but they will know that they are loved.

I remember disliking some teachers during high school because they were unusually tough on us kids. But when I matured I realized that these teachers had taught me how to think for myself and to be responsible. I'm doing the same for my children. Eventually I want them to be self-disciplined. Right now they are young and I discipline them frequently. This is because I am one hundred percent responsible for them and they are almost zero percent independent. As my kids grow older those percentages will reverse. That's why I love this wisdom from the Bible: "All discipline for the moment seems not to be joyful, but sorrowful; yet to those who have been trained by it, afterwards it yields the peaceful fruit of righteousness" (Hebrews 12:11, NASB). Though disciplining is tough on both parents and children (and a Red for most parents), I want my children to learn to make right choices for themselves.

Confidence will come in time and with practice, no matter what your GLC Profile. The two questions I ask myself concerning discipline are, "Am I being consistent?" and, "Do my children know that I love them?" As long as you can answer yes, you're doing well.

And speaking of consistency and confidence, you will have to develop those along with your husband. As part of your marriage, you and your husband need to discuss and plan together how your children will be disciplined. I know personally that this is an area of conflict and a source of irritation. Sometimes each of us thinks that we are right. However, it is not a matter of being right but of being a team, so as not to confuse the kids. "The saddest part about an uncoordinated approach to parenting is that the child is the loser. Never being quite sure which parent's rules are in effect because of a lack of consistency, he can't feel secure or confident. . . . The very first step to be taken is to establish rules that will be upheld consistently by both parents."[11]

And children need to know that you don't expect them to be perfect. Mistakes are OK; they are a part of life. Tell them that you love them, verbally, as much as they need to hear it. And when they do something wrong, explain to them why it is wrong. After resolving the issue, send them off with a hug, after telling them that you forgive them.

Ask for Your Child's Forgiveness

What about when you're the one who's wrong? I can remember the first time I had to say I was sorry to my then two-year-old daughter. It was hard to say "I'm sorry. Will you forgive me?" After all, she was only two and she'll forget about it. But I determined to start then. Her response was great: "That's OK Mommy," and gave me a big hug. And the release is wonderful in knowing that there is nothing between you, no barriers. Children readily forgive. And now that she is a little older, it is easier to say "Will you forgive me?" because I've done it before.

This also gives your own children an example to use in their own lives. I want my children to say they are sorry to one another and to other people. Even though, at the time, my son was only able to grunt, Nathan once went over to his sister, grunted while patting her on the head, and looked sad and sorry in his eyes and face. He still continues his habit of patting people on the head when he says "Sorry" to them.

Funtime and Playtime

There are a lot of fun aspects to being a parent. Think of all the fun that you have license to do because you bring a kid or two (or more) with you. It's great reliving what you did as a child or doing things you never did as a child. And nobody needs to know that you're not doing it just for your kids.

Having fun with your kids is one of the reasons Dave and I had them. But with our busyness and my everyday jobs of homemaker and mom, it's easy to let the fun part slip away. One mom that I know said once, "I feel as though I nag my kids a lot of the time. When I see them with the baby-sitter, they are having such a fun time. The sitter doesn't have to think about making supper and doing dishes and laundry. I decided to have more fun with my kids, to pretend I was just baby-sitting them and to ignore my other responsibilities." So she did it. She made time for her kids to be kids. She played with them and put the other priorities of life on the back burner.

You can do the same for your kids. Block off one or

two hours and devote it to the kids. Put the answering machine on and just play. Do something offbeat like serving sundaes for dinner. Take them to a kids' movie. Or let them buy a toy in the store for under a certain price. You can surprise them with a present for no special reason.

Our adventure in fun started out innocently enough. I wanted Hannah to have some dress up clothes because she seemed to enjoy it so much at a friend's house. I bought her a pair of clip-on earrings, a pair of shoes, a dress, a hat, and a couple of necklaces. I forgot Hannah's friends needed dress-up clothes too. So I bought another outfit. She loved it so much that I put it on her Christmas list. Relatives bought items and cleaned out their attic goodies. In the meantime, we kept our eyes open at tag sales, yard sales, and secondhand stores. Recently I bought, a good sized cabinet, about three feet high by a foot and a half deep, and four feet long. It is full. Last week I justified my spending to the owner of a secondhand clothes store as I bought a few more items. The previous time I dropped $30. You think me extravagant too? Yes, so what? As a mother it's my prerogative to be. Shouldn't life be extravagant and fun at times? The owner of the secondhand store reassures me, "She'll have wonderful memories of this." And you know what? So will I!

Benefits from Having Children

I have fun with my kids. Not all of the time, but I do enjoy them. Other than having fun with them, there are other benefits from having children. I'll tell you some of mine.

Some of my best learning has come as a result of

having children. I am awed by the honesty of kids. My daughter doesn't hesitate to answer, "No" to my husband's questions of, "Do you know what this means? Do you understand that?" Not many adults would do that. We have to protect our image and pretend that we know everything. In the process we miss out on some good learning opportunities.

Also, little kids live at a slower pace. A lot of times I want to say, "Hurry up, we're going to be late!" And most days I do. But kids take time to look at bugs and to notice airplanes. They live life to its fullest and enjoy each moment. I can learn from them to slow down and enjoy some of the moments too.

They are seeing some sights and events for the first time. It's wonderful to see these things through their eyes and thus relive parts of my own childhood. They are excited to see the first snowfall. They love to decorate the Christmas tree and to feel how soft a bunny rabbit is. For all of the work they are, they bring immeasurable joys. While we let the world revolve around them for a short while, we grow and mature. Our character is developed as we become less selfish. For many of us, we finally realize that the world doesn't revolve around us when we have children.

Love

If there is one word that expresses what your children need, it is love. And they need it from you, their mom. You will love them regardless of their strengths and weaknesses, regardless of how different they are from you or what they choose to do with their lives. You will be there for your children, loving them. That's a tall order to fill, but every loving mom wants to fill it. That's what you're aiming for.

Easy?

Is it easy to be a mom? No. It's never easy to be a parent. There are sacrifices of time and energy and freedom. You are not even assured of success. "Sacrifice is not convenient nor does it guarantee reward."[12] Even though results are not guaranteed, you and your husband are influencers. "Often we do not realize how much we are interacting or how much of a real effect our presence has on our children until we see them begin to imitate the behavior or espouse the values . . . of someone else who spends a lot of time with them or of us."[13] Parenting requires a lot of work. As Tim Kimmel puts it, "Effective parenting cannot be done by accident. We have to parent on purpose."[14] It takes time to be around kids—to listen to them, to praise them, to love them, to discipline them, and to encourage them.

There will be many times when you are tired and have other responsibilities, such as your husband, your house, your community, yourself, and perhaps paid work, pressing on you. But in everyday life, your simple decision to accept your children, set time aside for fun, discipline fairly, and encourage them in their potential GLC Profiles will show your kids that you love them.

Parenting is worth the expended effort. For with the unpleasant surprises that every child brings to a family come the joyous surprises that only that same child can bring.

How to Help Your Husband Relate to the Children

This involves three steps. One, knowing and accepting your Green (which may be no small task). Two, acknowledging that you and your husband have to temper your Green tendencies because of the situational realities. Three, quietly applying to your own life what you want to suggest to your husband. Carefully, tactfully point out what he might keep in mind while relating to your children.

If your husband is...

A Strategy Person

He may come across as a driver and pusher—the kind of person who wants to run up a mountain on a leisurely family hiking trip. The Strategy husband turns everything that he does into a competitive, beat-them situation.

Try pointing out that not every child is competitive. Together you need to allow your child to be who he or she is rather than pushing him or her to be a Strategy clone. Suggest to your husband that he intentionally lose a game when playing with the kids...or resist the temptation always to tell them what to do.

A Tasks Person

A Tasks husband may come across as a watchful hawk, noticing every flaw in speech, floors, dishes, clothes, etc. He can usually find something wrong with anything. And his "comments" may not be welcomed by people who worked themselves to the bone trying to do a good job.

A Tasks husband and father needs help looking at the positive side, not just the negatives. Try pointing out to him that your children may not be perfect writers or perfect room keepers! That is, it is OK that the family car not look spic and span when the kids are fidgeting in the back seat while waiting for someone.

An Ideas Person

An Ideas man may come across as reflective and contemplative. He needs time to turn things over in his mind. To him, learning and being creative is essential.

An Ideas husband needs help understanding that his children may not be whiz-bang students, as he was; or that they may not look forward to writing creative papers in sixth grade, and the like; or that the kids may want to spend Saturdays playing with the neighborhood kids rather than reading in the library.

A Relationships Person

A Relationships man may come across as the "socialite"— people, people, people. He would rather be with people than computers, books, or the household chores.

You can help a Relationships dad by making him aware of the fact that your children may happen to enjoy mathematics (and not necessarily turn into social misfits as a consequence); or that simple family gatherings may be boring to your children, rather than a satisfying and fun time for them; or that some children like to be alone or to do things alone.

Chapter 7

If You Are Single

—————◆—————

Jim Abbott is a pitcher for the California Angels. When we lived in California we saw him pitch against the Red Sox's ace Roger Clemens. Throughout the game we were amazed at Abbott, at his pitching and at his fielding. We'd seen a lot of baseball games but we'd never seen a one-handed pitcher. Abbott was born without his right hand. Still he decided to become a professional ballplayer. We watched his movements intently, trying to figure out how he put the glove on his hand, caught the ball, discarded his mitt, and threw the ball. We never did figure it out. Even his own catcher said of him, "You see him catch the ball, but you never see him put the glove on his hand."[1] In fact, "he is visible proof that what appears to some a limitation need not be."[2]

In a similar way I admire single moms, many of whom are living proof that not having a husband need not be a limitation. And I cannot figure out how they do it. When I was asked to include a chapter on single parenting in this book, my first reaction was, "How? I'm not qualified." I am like the spectator in the stands admiring Abbott's pitching and fielding, all the while wondering how he does it. Likewise, I am an onlooker into the lives of single parents. So this chapter is based not on my own experiences but from learning from other single moms.

I cannot say it enough: I am in awe of single parents. I have a husband who helps me at the end of many days when I am tired and haven't finished my long "To Do" list. We have two sets of hands, as my husband helps with the house and with the children.

"How do they do it?" is a question I often ask. It seems the most obvious question to ask.

But from my research I would change my key question to: "Why do they do it?" Jim Abbott's *Sports Illustrated* article gives us a clue: "Once you accept Abbott as a pitcher first, it's OK to marvel at how he does it."[3] If I may be allowed literary license, once you accept a single mom as a parent, it's OK to marvel at how she does it.

Parents First

Single parents are just that, parents first. If they love their children, they are committed to spending time with them and wanting the best for their kids. Often this exacts a higher personal cost in time and energy than a two-parent household. One mom said:

> It didn't seem there could be anything more difficult than two people juggling the demands of careers and children. But a year ago we split up, and now I know the demands of being a working couple

with children seem like a Caribbean cruise compared with the demands of being a *single* working parent of two preschoolers.[4]

But because of their motivation, many single moms are able to do their job of parenting. Out of necessity they have adapted and adjusted. I cannot fully understand how, as I've never been forced into the situation. But God does promise grace sufficient to meet our every need. "God is our refuge and strength, / A very present help in trouble" (Psalm 46:1, NASB).

There are many single parent moms whom I admire. Some have one child some of the time, and some have four all of the time. Many are divorced, a few are widows, and a few have never been married. In the case of the moms who have been widowed or divorced, it took a while for them to adjust. First there were distinct periods of initial shock, then adjustment, and eventually a sense of balance.

Initial Shock

Becoming a single parent is indeed a shock for many women. If you have become a single mom through a sudden death or an unexpected divorce or separation, the initial weeks and months can be almost overwhelming. Even for women who sensed a pending separation or divorce or whose husband had a prolonged illness leading to death, the changes in family structure and lifestyle can tend to be immense.

When I was twelve my parents divorced. Within one year my mom could no longer afford to make the mortgage payments on our home. We moved from a house to an inner-city apartment. This move necessitated a new neighborhood, new friends, and new schools. Our spending habits had to change; we no longer had a car, new clothes, vacations, or meals out. And the biggest change was that my dad was no longer readily available—our family life had changed. From the viewpoint of a child I understand the changes in a household that suddenly becomes headed by a single parent. But I could not then know the struggles that my mom and other women have experienced.

Broken Promises

Marriage vows are made in good faith. Yet what couple has not struggled in their marriage; has not questioned the vows that have been exchanged? I have struggled with the imperfections in my own marriage, as have many people that I know. What sets apart the marriage that lasts a lifetime? What enables a couple to continue, to struggle, and to make it work? In Chapter Five I explored that question a little bit, yet I don't have all the answers. I do know that rather than feel smug, I am grateful that my marriage has survived a time of testing. I fully realize that some husbands leave and get a divorce against the strongest desire of their wives. Also I acknowledge that abusive husbands must be left for the safety and sanity of the woman.

Regardless of the cause of divorce, the reality of the broken promise must be faced. There is often deep emotion involved in this area. One observant, sensitive writer penned, "I can see the pain that inevitably lurks behind the courage and the cheerfulness, that a broken promise has a long and ongoing history."[5] I'll look at some of the areas of life that are affected by a divorce or the death of a husband.

Lack of Support

"Being a single parent is like hitting a ball against a wall when you'd much rather have a game of tennis," writes author Carol Lynn Pearson in her book *One on the Seesaw.*[6] Suddenly there is no one to talk to and make decisions with. No one to discuss the kids' discipline, their school, and the many issues that having children inevitably raises. You are left to make numerous financial decisions on your own. Decisions range from where to live and how to spend woefully inadequate money to whether to fix an old car or buy a newer one. The decisions that need to be made, especially in the transition time, are numerous.

The particulars of your situation dictate your response—whether you and your husband worked well as a team in decision making before, your preparedness for his absence or death, the intensity of financial changes and lifestyle changes that need to be made. Relationships people will particularly miss interaction of this type; they enjoy teamwork and discussion. Tasks and Strategy people tend to be less overwhelmed by making decisions as they functioned more independently even when married. Ideas people will tend to focus on the aspects of the ideal marriage and regret the broken promises.

Your adjustment can also be eased by the help of others. If you have a good friend with whom to discuss critical issues, you will do better. Also, if you are able to find assistance with household maintenance and car repairs, that will help immensely. I like the words of one single parent, "Being a parent—especially a single parent—means you *can't* do it all alone. And if you're lucky, you don't have to."[7] I hope you are able to have a support team for your needs.

Self Identity

In each stage of my life, I've asked myself the question, "Who am I, really?" Times of change make me question and re-evaluate myself and my priorities. You may have been thrust into the role of single parent and not wanted it. One woman said, "I didn't know where to turn. I had no handles. I didn't know what I was going to do."[8]

While I believe that every woman needs to know her lifetime dreams and who she is, a single mom has an urgent need to know them for at least two reasons. First, her lifestyle has been turned upside down and the regular lifestyle has been temporarily disrupted, causing emotional upheaval. Second, she may have to support her family alone. Chapters Three and Four can help you begin to plan for your future. The Appendices also contain valuable information for career selection.

Stress Factors

Death or divorce are two of the most stressful times in a person's life, according to stress experts. Listed below are some stressful changes that may accompany single parenthood. Also listed are the stress points associated with that change. In a one-year period, more than 200 stress points is cause for concern.

Stress Factors[9]

Death of spouse	100
Divorce	73
Marital separation	65
Marital reconciliation	45
Sexual Difficulties	39

Major change in finances 38
In-law troubles 29
Major change in work 20
New residence 20
Change to new school 20

The statistics show that the average woman's standard of living decreases 73 percent after divorce, while the average man's standard of living increases 43 percent.[10] Thus, you may be faced with the possibility of facing many stress conditions at once.

Needy Children, Needy Mom

I can understand the needs of a child after a divorce. I've been one. Yet at the same time, I can see that a single mom is at her neediest soon after the change. Whether she wants to or not, she must deal with the changes and emotions of the worst time in her life.

Most often a single parent is a mom. In fact, the statistics show that 90 percent of women have custody of their children.[11] One definition of joint custody I found says that "the mother gets custody of the child when the *child* needs someone, while the father gets custody when *he* needs someone."[12] I hope that you are able to ease up on yourself during this critical time, knowing that "it is also difficult for one who is emotionally drained and thirsty to give continually to those around."[13]

Moving Forward

"When you can let go of the past and redirect your view to the present and the future, then you are in control of defining your important new roles."[14] That is a very true statement from one woman who has done it. I am able to move forward when I realize that even though life is not fair, I must move forward. One single mom wrote that you "can't unscramble an egg."[15] But in my own life I know I try to do this. It happens when I dwell on the "if only's" and "why me's." Instead you need to concentrate on the "what do I have to do to make my life work?" Only then will you be well on your way forward. Though becoming single is not always the mom's choice, single parents can accept that life can and will go on. Moving forward begins when the pain of a circumstance no longer blocks your ability to think clearly and take concrete steps.

Yet before you can move forward in any aspect of your life in which you experience deep loss, you must grieve. The grieving is not only for the loss of your husband through death or divorce, but extends to all areas of your life. You have lost a companion, a support, a confidant, a lover, and a father for your children. For many single parents the loss associated with the breaking of the marriage promise is tragic. Not only that but you have lost the family structure that you were accustomed to. In effect, your whole world has changed—the outward lifestyle as well as the inner heart changes that the world rarely sees. I attended a conference recently in which a speaker said, "Grief cannot be postponed indefinitely." In your heart only you know if you have really grieved to satisfy your inner self.

After the initial transition, memories can spark reminders of your ex-husband, good and bad times—bringing back once again the intense feelings you thought were under control. But those feelings will pass. One mom put it this way: "The pain of any loss lessens and at times disappears entirely. Yet it resurfaces briefly at unexpected moments as vividly as ever." The pain never fully goes away, but it lessens considerably and it doesn't have to control you. Many experiences in life are seasonal:

> There is an appointed time for everything.
>
> And there is a time for every event under heaven—
>
> A time to tear down, and a time to build up.
>
> A time to weep, and a time to laugh;
>
> A time to mourn, and a time to dance.
>
> —Ecclesiastes 3:1, 3-4 (NASB)

Choices

Single moms can make choices to help themselves and their children to re-establish a new family balance.

Choosing to Forgive

Forgiveness is not usually a one time act. In my own life with deep hurts, I've needed to forgive and reforgive as new events have resparked my initial anger. When I view the future shaped by the pain and losses of the past, I can become angry all over again. When this happens I need to forgive, again, for my own sake. For single moms this is also true—the pain and loss are felt for a long time, perhaps a lifetime. A well worded piece of wisdom from Savonarola is, "Do not forgive and forget; forgive and remember. . . . The only true forgiveness is to remember and still forgive."[16]

Therefore, forgiveness is not shrugging off the past and the person who has hurt you. Rather, forgiveness "sees the wrong fully, but then chooses to set it aside and focus on it no more."[17] Forgiving someone does more than let that person off the hook; it frees you up. Your energy is no longer directed toward revenge, hatred, or getting even. You are free to live your own life, concentrating your limited energy into your children and your new lifestyle.

Choosing to Meet Your Children's Needs

When you forgive your ex-husband, you have taken an immense beginning to meeting your children's needs. How? You no longer hold anything against him. This sets the atmosphere for your children to remain loving their dad; you will not belittle their father. For even though your intimate relationship with him is over, theirs never is and never should be. In fact, "children keenly miss even a bad father."[18] Your choice gives them the security that they desperately need and makes their disrupted life more manageable. It doesn't tangle them up in your adult conflicts; it allows them to remain in childhood and not to be prematurely thrust into the adult world.

Words can mean a lot. Don't underestimate the power of words. In fact, you may want to use these words with your children:

- "It [the divorce or death] is not your fault."
- "I wish we could spend more time together."
- "I know it's not easy, but I'm here with you."
- "How are you doing?"
- "How are you feeling?"
- "I love you."

Words like these spoken by you can help your children more than you know.

Choosing to Let Others Help

Your close friends and relatives might not know how to help you. Or they might not even know how to ask you if you need help. They may drop passing hints like, "If there's anything I can do, just let me know." Many people need to be directed in their help. When someone mentions something casually, you might respond with specific ways in which they could assist. The following statements are meant to get you thinking.

- ♦Fridays are particularly tough after a long work week. Could you bring a meal over this Friday?

- ♦I could use some time to myself to go shopping. Would you watch the kids for me Saturday afternoon for a couple of hours?

- ♦I know you shop at the food warehouse store. Sometimes I could use some stock up items from there. Would you mind picking some things up for me?

- ♦I never was one to work on the house or the car. Would you mind if I called you when I have a problem with either of them?

- ♦I could use a listening ear.

Choosing to Set Realistic Expectations

"Scale down your expectations" and "make a pact with yourself to do what is possible and let other expectations go."[19] This is good advice for all moms who need to preserve sanity, energy, and precious family time, but it is particularly great for single moms. With all of their many responsibilities, single moms can feel guilty and so tend to overdo in other areas to try to compensate.

Guilt and the dreaded "should" can be your worst enemies. Guilt can arise because you regret not being a traditional family, because you may have to work for pay, or because you don't have the time, energy, or patience with the kids that you used to. Ease up on expectations so that you can spend precious time with your kids and yourself. The next chapter will detail ways, task by task, to make housework more manageable, and thus relieve a lot of the guilt. Chapter Eleven covers the ways and reasons to say no (and saying no is particularly good for time-pressed single moms).

Choosing to Believe You *Are* a Family

"It's blue," my two-year-old son says.

"No, it's really red," I correct.

Almost exasperated, he defends: *"No! It's blue!"*

There is just no sense arguing. His mind is made up. I think, *Have it your way. I can't win this argument.* Somewhere, somehow Nathan incorrectly learned that the color red was blue.

Like my son, it's all too easy to skirt the obvious facts. Single parents often do this with the meaning of being a family.

You may not feel like a family because of the changes in your family. Maybe you are clinging to the falsehood that a family can only be what you had before. In that case you need to redefine your family, acknowledging that your new grouping is indeed a family.

Redefine Family

One mom who wrote about her divorce relates, "Now that it's just the two of us, will we ever feel like a family again?" Through her struggles she came to say, "even if there were only two of us now, we were still a family. . . . Lord, help Kelly and me establish traditions of our own."[20]

Establishing traditions need not be time-consuming or elaborate. Some of the traditions we have depend upon a season or a holiday; others are just times of celebrating. Here are some of my family's traditions:

♦ Cutting down our own tree for Christmas

♦ On vacation days, Christmas morning, birthdays, and celebrations we have a big breakfast of scrambled eggs, sausage, cantaloupe, juice, and bagels with cream cheese.

♦ When it snows or it's cold outside we make homemade cocoa and sit by the fireplace watching a video, reading, or playing a board game.

♦ Summertime finds us out and going—soaking up New England's too-short season. Picnics are big with us, so our picnic basket is almost always ready to go (prepacked with plates, cups, silverware, napkins, and tablecloth).

♦ Birthdays are special events—the whole day is spent doing fun activities, such as going out to eat, seeing movies, and having playtime.

♦ We're always looking for something to celebrate. A homemade (or store-bought) cake with candles and a congratulations card are easy to round up.

Our traditions are nothing exciting or earth-shattering, but they give security to our kids (whether one or two parents are around) and uniqueness to our family. One mom wrote, "Traditions are powerful framers of our definition of who we are as a family.... Change some of the traditions to suit the needs of the new family structure."[21]

How were our traditions established? No one is quite sure—we kind of tried some ideas and the ones that we liked we kept and refined. Since all families are different, you can get other ideas from books like *Let's Make A Memory* by Gaither and Dobson, or *The Big Book of Christmas Ideas* for some brainstorming fuel. We are sure of one thing: These little acts, rituals almost, say that we are family. They help us *feel* like a family.

No one has a monopoly on feeling like a family. A two-parent household with kids is no more a family than a single-parent household with kids. I believe, as one single mom wrote, "We're all of us, whatever shape our family takes, worth respecting, supporting, celebrating."[22] Do you believe her?

I'm glad that we are a family that likes to celebrate one another's achievements and accomplishments. My daughter Hannah performed in her first ballet recital last year. We threw a party with the works—cake, cards, relatives, and a small present to commemorate the occasion. When this book was accepted for publication, Hannah fashioned a piece of paper into a blue first prize ribbon. On it she wrote, "happy first book." Times like these melt hearts and mold them together into a family. Two parents are not a requirement for a family; moldable, open hearts are a prerequisite. So we can choose to believe that we are family, taking decisive action to form the little but significant ties that join individuals into a family. How will you decide? Will you be like my son Nathan who refused to face the facts, or will you choose to believe that yours is a family?

A Right Focus

Abbott can pitch. He's adapted to his one-handed functioning—he had to to play the game. Single moms can adapt to not having a husband for themselves and a father for their children. If you want to be in the game, to be a parent, you can adapt.

You have my full admiration. For while I as a parent face many of the same struggles and joys in raising children, loving children and carving out a family niche, "a single parent knows that the next shift is never coming in."[23]

That day in California, Clemens lost the game to Abbott. The deciding factor was the pitching hand, not the fielding hand. Abbott could have grown accustomed to the words, "He couldn't succeed because he had no right hand."[24] Yet his lifestyle shows that he made other choices based on the belief that he could pitch. Don't buy the lie that you aren't able to parent effectively because you are missing a "hand." Concentrate on your pitching hand, the one that you do have and can use—you.

PART FOUR

Setting Realistic Expectations in Housework

Chapter 8

A Clean Sweep

---◆---

"What did you do today?" my husband asked as he returned home from a day at the office. Our first child was about four months old. He walked in and saw the results of a tired mommy spending a day with a sick baby. There were dishes piled in the sink, there was clutter everywhere, and the mail was still in the mail slot. *How could I begin to tell him what this day has been like?* I pondered.

In my mind I went over the events of the day. I'd breast-fed the baby four (or was it five?) times. I'd changed nine diapers and washed out two baby outfits because she had power-pooped on them. I changed my own clothes once when she spit up on me. How could I tell him about my day? And did he really want to know?

I know that sounds familiar to most of you. Are you laughing because it was a while ago and your husband never asks that question again, or are you crying because it happened this week? In any case, it's a common scene in American households with babies or small children. My husband doesn't ask that question anymore. Instead he tests the waters first by asking, "How was your day?"

The House Will Come to Order

How can I be home all day and have the house look like vandals came and ransacked the place? Sometimes it is because of exhaustion from taking care of ill children. But many times my house looks messy and cluttered merely because of my regular activities.

What can a mother do about the chaos? *Should* she do anything about it?

Getting More Organized

For most people, a list of strategies doesn't work, at least not in the long run. *The Messies' Manual* was a book chosen for discussion at the mothers' group that I attend. I didn't even bother to read that book because it is all about developing an orderly and consistent *method* for cleaning. As an Ideas person, I would enjoy reading the book and learning a new method; it would be fun implementing this method until I learned how to do it. But after that it would be boring and monotonous and, well, just a plain Red.

However, Tasks people would really love *The Messies' Manual* and put it to good use. Setting up systems, standards, and checklists are Greens for them. The other GLC Profiles—Relationships and Strategy—would not use those methods consistently for any length of time.

Maintaining a Positive Attitude

Positive thinking doesn't work for me either. Like the little "I think I can" train straining to get over the mountain, it works for the short term but not for day-in and day-out work, year after year. A positive attitude only carries me through the lunch dishes. After that event, I'm positive that I hate housework.

Considering It As a Job

I used to read and think that if I just got more positive feedback from my husband (certainly not from my kids), I'd be able to muster enough emotional energy to keep my house clean and orderly—all the time. Positive feedback could be in the form of verbal praise from my husband; something like, "The house looks good lately, we could invite anyone in at any time." Or it could be in the form of written expectations and evaluations of my housework based on what my husband and I felt was important. Or it could be monetary, as in cash payments for my work by the hour or by the job. These suggestions seem silly when I write them out, but this is exactly what I've thought about housework.

At times I've said to my husband, "Where's my forty-eight?" A forty-eight means a promotion, a title of honor at his company. Doing my housework is hard, overwhelming work and I oftentimes feel that I get no rewards. Yet, that's not my husband's fault. It's my Green, my strength, that is out of sync with housecleaning.

Blaming it on the Kids

My children are messy because they are young. They have bad days. They spill things. They spew their toys all over the house just as Mount Saint Helens spewed ash over North America. They're home for a good part of the day. All of these reasons translate into a good-sized mess by the end of the day. So, I console myself with this poem:

Cleaning and scrubbing can wait 'til
   tomorrow...

For babies grow up, we've learned to our
   sorrow...

So quiet down cobwebs...

Dust, go to sleep...

I'm rocking my baby and babies don't keep.

—Anonymous[1]

I love that little poem. I use it to justify my lack of fervor for attending to my house. Yes, my children are young and time does pass quickly. But as they get older, I'll come up with new excuses. By then I may be working longer hours or more involved in community activities, and again I'll be "too busy" for housework. I may as well just face it now. I don't like housework, I never will enjoy doing housework, it's a *Red*. For the rest of my life my house will probably be unkempt, untidy, and messy. I can only hope it'll look a little better as the kids get older because there won't be Cheerios on the floor at all times.

Let's Get Real

Getting more organized, maintaining a positive attitude, considering house cleaning as a job, and blaming it on the kids doesn't work. Rather, what we need to be is honest with ourselves. It's OK not to like housework. It's OK if your house is not as clean as mine. Is it OK if my house is dirtier than yours?

My friend Sue is a perfect example of this, and she won't be embarrassed to admit it either. She and her husband do fine with her level of housework. I think we'd say, "I couldn't live like that," but it works for them. They're doing well, it doesn't bother them, their kids are happy and they are happy. Now isn't this much better than being uptight about the house all day? I think it is. Sue is a relationships person and that's where she spends a lot of her time. Since it works for Sue and her family, how can we tell Sue what she should be doing in the area of house cleaning? Sue and my friend Nan are similar when it comes to housework. Before company arrives for dinner or a party, they do a massive house-cleaning. The job gets done, unconventionally, but it gets done. I just hope they both continue to invite people over.

Again, I bring us back to the traffic light. For me housework is a definite *Red*. I don't enjoy doing it, and I'm not good at it. But that does not mean that it does not get done. I'm not talking about throwing away respon-sibilities; I'm talking about making them fit to who I am, while still taking care of my family. Again, I rely on my values when I am faced with Red tasks that must be done. The Bible says, "She looks well to the ways of her household, / And does not eat the bread of idleness" (Proverbs 31:27 NASB). I am talking about establishing family standards so that everyone is comfortable with where they live, but doable standards for me so I don't go nuts just keeping the house clean.

There are everyday chores that must get done, such as dishes, a few meals, and picking up the clutter at night. I tend to do a blitz on cleaning my house. If I'm lucky, once a week I go through the place with vacuum, mop, and dusting rag and do a good job. But my house is not your house, and yes, my house is livable, but it's not squeaky clean or nitpicky neat. If you're cringing, there are at least a couple of possibilities. One is that maintain-ing a house is a Green for you or possibly a Yellow, and that's fine. Then perhaps you should spend time on your home, more time than I. The second possibility is that you've not thought of lowering your housekeeping standards despite the fact that you do not enjoy doing housework. In other words, you feel you should have your house clean no matter what. There's that "should" word again. It pops up a lot for us moms.

"Does anyone enjoy doing housework?" you may be asking in disbelief. Yes, my friend Sandy does. She enjoys the cleaning—the whole bit of it—and the satisfaction she has when she sees a job well done. In her stage of kids, however, she has had to lower her standards (she has boys age 6 and 4 and twin girls age 2). But she intends to get going in full swing again when the kids are older.

What about you? Which of the following statements best describes you? Do you see yourself in any of these statements?

1. I like things in order. I like to spend the time to have my house be clean and organized. I have an established system or would like to set up an established system for cleaning. I don't want things to just *look* clean, I want them to *be* clean. It drives me crazy when the house is dirty or when I can't find something I need. I want my house organized.

2. I'd like my house to be cleaner but I won't stop inviting my friends over just because it's not spotless. My friends like me for who I am. I'd rather be playing with the kids or talking with a friend than cleaning.

3. I blitz through doing my housework in order to have time to do other things. Honestly, I like to do it with speed and a lot of the times I miss spots on dishes. I like to get it done fast. There is no fulfillment for me in a clean house.

4. To me, housework is boring. I do it when I have to, but I don't enjoy it. I'm not much on cleaning for the sake of cleaning, but I want my house to look nice because I want to use it as a backdrop to showcase my art. I do housework more for looks than for cleanliness.

Tasks women would most likely identify with the first statement. The second statement would be indicative of a Relationships person, the third of Strategy, and the fourth of Ideas. The GLC Profiles for housecleaning are easy to remember—for Tasks it is Green and for all the rest it is a Red, though Relationships people can consider it a Yellow if they're doing it to help people. Perhaps now you know why you love housework or hate it!

Before leaving this topic I offer a few words of consolation to Tasks women who like to set up systems to clean. You can become (or maybe have already become) a discouraged cleaner because the order you've brought to your home disintegrates into chaos too soon. Be encouraged: As your children get older, your home will tend to stay organized longer, lessening the frustration of not being able to keep up.

Strategies to Help You

Set Realistic Expectations

Based on the above ratings of Red, Yellow, and Green, what should your expectations be for house cleaning? If it's a Red, expect not to like doing it, expect yourself not to do a great job, expect yourself to procrastinate, expect the job to take twice as long as it should, and expect yourself to be drawn to other activities instead of cleaning. Give yourself a break and think about relaxing your standards or consider other options.

What Works for You?

Use a system that works for you. When I can't stand it any longer, I clean. This works for us because my husband and I are in agreement with the cleanliness level of our house. He realizes that there is only so much time in each day and I want to spend those hours with the kids and writing tasks. Our system, or lack of a system, works for our family.

The friends I wrote about earlier do a blitz cleaning right before company comes over. This is unlike the Tasks women who want a methodical system; they could use ideas from *The Messies' Manual*, develop their own system, or use another system. Ask yourself and other family members, "Is this working? If not, what can we do to make it work?"

What about Your Husband?
What about the Kids?

As women, our lives are intricately woven tapestries, I think more so than men's. In many cases, it is the woman of the house who does much of the cooking, cleaning, laundry, and shopping, along with taking care of the kids. There is still a wide gap between women and men when it comes to housework. In fact, "two-thirds [of women] do all the shopping, laundry and bill paying; over 40 percent do all the cooking and cleaning."[2] Our modern men are much better than most of our dads, though. Our husbands usually change diapers, help feed the baby, play with the kids, take them for walks— all of which was virtually foreign to men a mere thirty years ago.

The GLC division of labor would divide jobs based on a person's Greens; whoever is best suited for the job would do it. If no one likes doing a particular job, whoever is the least busy will do that job or some other agreed-upon method. In our house, whoever is the most tired gets reprieve from jobs. This is not how it plays out all the time in our home, but that's what we're aiming at. If you have a husband who equally distributes the house jobs with you, as well as the kids, then you are truly lucky—only a small percentage of husbands do.

At our kids' ages (preschool) it is oftentimes easier and quicker not to let them help. It takes a while to train children. But in just a couple of years they will be able to work around the house, and it will be good for them to do so. In a few years we will reap the benefits of training our children. Hannah and Nathan will soon be helping me with my Red housekeeping responsibilities.

Hire Help

We've neglected, thus far, to consider the possibility of help with the housework. Perhaps someone could come in and clean your house thoroughly every week or two? Do I detect laughter? I, too, would love to exercise this option, but we do not choose to spend money this way. We have higher priorities, such as replacing our second car before it is condemned to the junk heap, and saving for our kids' college education. Then there are always dance lessons, new clothes for growing kids, and the list goes on. But some women are in a position to consider hiring domestic help. If housework is a Red, why not consider it? If our finances ever change, it's on my "I'll consider it strongly" list.

We've Only Just Begun

There is more to running a household than cleaning. Homemaking includes cleaning, making repairs/fixing things, decorating, cooking, entertaining, paying bills/ managing finances, and shopping. I'll examine how each of those jobs meshes with your strengths. Whatever your profile, you will enjoy some jobs and dislike others.

Making Repairs/Fixing Things

Let's not be sexist in reverse here. Just as men are capable of cleaning house, women are capable of making repairs and fixing those very many things that break. The woman who likes to repair things is mostly in the GLC Green of Tasks. She will be thorough and diligent, taking her time in making repairs.

Rather than make repairs and improvements herself, the Strategy woman enjoys hiring out jobs and over-seeing the work being done. She is not picky about perfection but is interested in observable results. She will be irritated if jobs aren't completed on schedule.

An Ideas woman will make repairs to household items in the clothing, fabric, and wallpapering areas that tend to be decorative and artsy as well as practical. She will also want to restore those items, but she prefers to start from scratch and make her own rather than correct mistakes or breaks.

Initially, an Ideas woman will be enthusiastic as she learns how to do repairs. But her enthusiasm will wane because she would rather learn a subject and then move on to something else than do the task itself.

Relationships women will do some repairs if they are able to do them with or for someone else.

Decorating, Sewing, and Doing Crafts

The GLC Profile that shines in the area of decorating is Ideas. An Ideas woman has a vision for a home, either new or used, and is likely to design her own house. She is crafty and creative in doing things with cloth, making curtains, and in upholstering furniture. She is better still at creating something from nothing. She may design her own stencils, weave blankets, and make baskets. She does it because she likes to make original items, not because of the attention her work will bring her. She's like Martha Stewart, a nationally known decorator, cook, designer, and author. In fact, an Ideas woman will not know when to stop; she will always be making items for her house and adding to them. And she won't be in a hurry because she loves the process.

Some Ideas women like to learn how to do and master skills such as wallpapering and refinishing furniture. They enjoy the learning, but they do not like to do such tasks for a long time. They do well to plan a spot in their homes for their many books and magazines, as well as a place to write and think away from their kids' voices.

A Tasks woman likes the job of wallpapering, stenciling, and other work if she can do it primarily by herself. Her strength is not in picking out colors or designs but in doing the work. She will want everything done correctly and will spend the extra time measuring so that it will be correct. She may find herself redoing things because it just doesn't look right. Because she likes to improve things, an older home is more her niche. However, she will be frustrated if there is not enough money or time to refurbish an older house.

Relationships women will tend to decorate and plan their home to have a lot of people in their homes. This could mean a large kitchen and a large living room. Many Relationships women enjoy doing some decorating, especially if done with a friend. There are a few with this style who are not afraid of experimentation in their homes. They are likely to have offbeat, unique items displayed in clever ways throughout their homes. The common thread uniting the rooms will be the differences. These few Relationships people make each room special and unique, using items they bought while visiting a friend in Pennsylvania Dutch country or from their great-aunt Alice or from their mom.

Strategy women like to see progress right away. They like fast results; painting and other projects with visible results are good. Mostly, they prefer to hire someone whom they supervise. They dislike loose ends.

Cooking Three Meals a Day

A Tasks woman will enjoy the details of cooking. She will (almost) always go by a recipe and carefully follow the directions. Some Tasks women will even level off the flour when measuring, like they taught us to in junior high cooking class. She likes to cook alone whenever possible. She will be discouraged if she cannot find the proper ingredients and pan at the store, and disappointed if her result does not look like the cookbook picture. She may also like to make calculated changes to an existing recipe. She'll change a little amount of this spice or add this new ingredient or bake it a little longer at a lower temperature. She wants to improve a recipe or a method but she will usually have to start with something concrete.

An Ideas woman, however, is creative and can start from just an idea of what would be good together and do it. She might keep a recipe in her head and never write it down. She particularly likes cake decorating and making fancy hors d'oeuvres, where her creativity can shine. For her, variety is indeed the spice of life. She likes to experiment and try new recipes and new foods. How can she learn about how other people live? She can cook their food and experience it. She may try recipes not ordinarily cooked by others. Everyday cooking bores her.

A Strategy woman has difficulty shining in this area; it's not challenging enough. She will not be able to compete with anyone. This is in her Red. She may enjoy a short-term challenge such as being stranded in the wilderness, having to hunt for her own food and cook it with wet wood and no matches. But 365 days a year, three meals a day is a Red.

A Relationships woman will go out of her way to prepare a special dish for you. She wants you to appreciate her efforts. And if the dish flops, she wants you to say you appreciate her effort. She enjoys talking to someone while she is cooking.

Entertaining and Hosting

The most natural hostesses are the Relationships women. It is second nature for them to welcome friends or strangers into their homes. Cleanliness is not important to this style, but hospitality and meeting needs are. They simply enjoy spending time with people. It doesn't have to be fancy or elaborate, though at times they will make it such. No other GLC style has such ease with people.

Ideas women will ask a lot of questions as they are entertaining, in an effort to learn. Also, when they invite people over they will tend to display their handicrafts more than entertain.

Tasks women may not like to spend a lot of time with people, so they don't entertain much.

Strategy women like quick, to-the-point types of get-togethers. Long chats and relationship-building are not natural for them.

Relationships women are the ones who really try to meet people's needs and build relationships with people.

My idea of entertaining is a cross between Ideas and Tasks. I ask a lot of questions to learn from people. Also, I like to show off all the work we've done renovating our old house, along with its old furnishings. I'm not that good at meeting people's needs, at making them feel at ease and at knowing the right things to say at the right time. I do not feel at ease in entertaining frequently. Why? It's not my Green. It's probably a pale Yellow. I entertain to build relationships with other people because I value people.

I look at others who entertain much more frequently than I do; I note the ease with which they mix talk with serving and laughter; and sometimes I say to myself, "That looks so easy, I should be able to do that." But I can't and just never will be able to do that. That is their strength, not mine.

Paying Bills and Managing Finances

Tasks women tend to find a niche in this aspect of running a home. They like to work with data and to keep track of records. They enjoy developing an orderly system, keeping accurate records, reconciling accounts, and calculating how much to save for purchases. These jobs are all important to operating a household and will be relatively easy for Tasks women with the proper training.

For years my husband handled our finances and bill paying. It drove him crazy. He'd forget to pay bills. For me it's somewhat easier, as tasks is my Yellow. Why did my husband wait so long to hand over the finances? Because in our peer groups, the man was expected to handle the finances because he is a man. We say no to that expectation now.

However, both partners in a marriage should know how to do finances, know the general financial outlook for the family, and where the money is being spent. Once a year, usually at tax time, we revise our budget and financial policies. My husband makes the bottom-line decisions. Throughout the year I handle the details of the finances because I am the one most suited to do it.

Shopping

As in other areas, women differ a lot in the area of shopping. Tasks people are bargain hunters. They don't mind items that need to be repaired or fixed. Second-hand stores, yard sales, and wholesale stores are a dream come true for them. While shopping, they tend to use a list and stick to it. They like to shop alone, not with the kids. Tasks people are coupon-clipping maniacs. They love sales, especially going-out-of-business sales. They can stretch a pound of meat like no other TLC style.

Strategy women are less concerned about the money saved. They want to save time. They dislike shopping, especially food shopping once or twice a week. They want to shop with speed. As such, one-stop shopping is made for them. It's wonderful to have a pharmacy, video rental, produce, meat, bakery, dry cleaning, photo developing, and everything in one store. They are also fond of mail-order catalogues, which save lots of time.

Relationships women can savor the shopping experience. They like to chat with their friends as they shop for clothes and household items. They are more interested in spending time with people than in price or speed. They tend not to get organized enough to use coupons consistently or to seek out the sales. They will not mind, usually, bringing their kids with them to the grocery store.

Ideas women like antique and specialty shops. They especially enjoy craft stores, craft shows, and fabric shops as well as gourmet, ethnic, and specialty food stores. Additionally, they love secondhand and new book stores. Everyday shopping is especially dull to them and they don't like to shop with the kids.

The Significance of Housework

Home is where the heart is. It's also where the dishes, the laundry, the cooking, and the cleaning hang out. Housework can eat up vast amounts of time. It never gets all done; there is always more to do. It's like a black hole.

I've decided that my time and life are not going to get sucked into the housekeeping black hole. However, if your Green is in the jobs of housework, you have a valid reason for getting sucked into it. As for me and my housework, I tend to put it on the back burner. I feel like the woman writer who said, "I know I could be doing more housework . . . but there's no end to it. Sometimes I feel a little guilty when people come over. . . . Besides, I'm starting to get work published, and my family's content with things as they are. What more could anyone want?"[3]

The book *In Search of Excellence* expounds a pervasive attitude in our culture. We are encouraged to pursue excellence in all things. However, pursue excellence in your Greens, otherwise you will set yourself up for frustration because your imposed standards will be impossible for you to maintain over the long haul. Give yourself permission not to do all things well.

This advice is particularly important for the Strategy mom. She tends to be the most unfulfilled of all of the GLC Profiles when it comes to domestic responsibilities. She has little, perhaps nothing, to do around the house that is in her Green. The Strategy mom must be motivated by her value judgments when doing household work; she must see that she is providing a valuable service to her family. The Strategy woman will tend to rely heavily on her Yellow to help her through motherhood. So I recommend rereading this chapter for jobs that fit your Yellow. Concentrating your efforts on those homemaking responsibilities will help.

The Strategy mom is also likely to feel a strong pull to pursue her Green away from the home because she is the only style that has little at home to feel good about. For all of the other GLC Profiles there are some shining glimmers of hope in the form of greens. For example, Ideas women can decorate, sew, do crafts, garden, arrange flowers, and make items, collecting ideas from many sources; Tasks women can clean and organize, as well as pay bills and arrange the finances; and Relationships women can spend time with their husband and kids. The Strategy woman has no such outlet.

If there is one way we could help each other as mothers, it would be to have tolerance for one another's housekeeping standards. Housework is not a matter of life and death. It's not nearly as vital as our relationships with our children and our husbands. And it is not a reflection of character but of gifts.

In my life I sense the perfect housekeeper barriers come crashing down when I admit that my house isn't very clean and that it's usually pretty cluttered. Relief floods over a mom's face as I tell her this. It's as if I've just given this woman permission not to have her house clean at all times. She is able to open up and admit that her house is not the cleanest and that she really doesn't enjoy house cleaning.

When all is said and done about housework, will you determine what you will do based on your Greens? This area is one in which you can really decide what your standards will be and what amount of work you will do. Since it's important, I'll repeat it again: Yellow can be done for a short time and you'll do a reasonably good job at it; Red should be avoided for long periods of time. Expect not to like Reds at all and allow your standards there to be low. Tasks women are the people who enjoy spending vast amounts of time in these areas. Strategy moms dislike most of these jobs. Relationships and Ideas women can find some fulfillment in homemaking jobs.

While a Tasks woman may choose to spend oodles of time here, "Streamline your housework in order to have time for writing,"[4] replacing the word "writing" with *your* lifetime dream.

PART FIVE

Setting Realistic Expectations in Work

Chapter 9

What Works for You

―――――◆―――――

She stands alone facing her accusers. In her arms she cradles her four-year-old's rag doll. The circles under her eyes are the prize that a new baby often brings. Uncompassionately oblivious to her, the professor begins the oral exam by reprimanding her. "You're late, Ms. Murdoch."

Ms. Murdoch's face does not reveal the intended sting of the word "Ms." and the use of her maiden name. She responds, "I know. I threw my husband a surprise party for extra credit."

Apparently not a sufficient answer, the professor refutes her, "Extra credit for a seminar in woman's studies? I don't think so. *(Pause.)* Let me ask you this. *(Pause.)* What are you planning to do with your life?"[1]

Sometimes art, like that *thirtysomething* episode, imitates my life. Since the recent birth of her second child,

Hope Murdoch Stedman feels as though she is barely making it as a wife and mother. Ever feel like that some days? And to compound her life she receives a "so what have you been doing since you graduated from Princeton?" questionnaire. It makes her think about her past, the long ago before kids when life was simpler. It makes her reflect on what she expects from herself and what society, especially her peers, seems to demand she do and be. I've received those dreaded questionnaires from my graduating college, Worcester Polytechnic Institute. I felt great when I could write down a title and job responsibilities, especially something as prestigious as Quality Control Manager. But now that I am mostly a mom, I cringe when I receive them. These questionnaires make me want to return to work, to do something society values, or, if not that, to make up some grandiose accomplishment that would impress my former peers.

Sometimes art, like *thirtysomething*, reflects our times. Today roles are not as clearly defined as they once were. Though the show *thirtysomething* has come and gone, the attitude that a woman is not good enough as "just a housewife" remains. These are times of confusion.

Three concepts have to be identified to understand how a mother feels about her role. The first is the *Mommy Wars*, the second is the *Status Hierarchy*, and the third is the *Earning Hierarchy*.

Mommy Wars

"What do you do all day?" asks a mom who works for pay of a mom who stays at home.

"How can you leave your children all day with someone else while you go off to work for that new mini-van?" asks a stay-at-home mom of a work-for-pay mom. And so goes the mommy war. Mostly, the arguments are not that explosive; not that direct. Yet there are tensions between the two groups.

Sometimes that tension spills out into all-out warfare as the two polarized views tug at you and at the conflicting feelings inside you as a person and as a mother. That is what the mommy war is all about. Each side attempts to enlist you on their side. The two polarized groups will be called the feminists and the traditionalists, for lack of better names.

The feminists state their case like this: "I am a person in my own right and I need to work. I'd go crazy at home all day. Women stayed at home all day with their children only in the agricultural days. There was so much more for a woman to do at home then that they had to. For sheer economic survival, the woman needed to do farm chores, labor intensive meal preparations, and household tasks too numerous to mention. She also taught her children at home as well as made the family's clothing. And today we know that the divorce rate is so high, I want to be prepared in case this should happen to me. I want to be prepared to support myself if I have to."

The traditionalists contend: "I do not just stay at home. I get actively involved with my children, spending much time nurturing them, playing with them, reading to them, and teaching them. I bake and make home cooked meals. I enjoy staying at home. I don't watch soap operas or do nothing all day. The time I spend with my children while they are young is a priceless investment in their future. I'm willing to make sacrifices for my children's sake. And I try not to worry about the possibility of divorce; I put it in the back of my mind."

Unfortunately not only do both sides of the argument believe that they have the correct answer, they both want to convert you to their way of thinking. However, there are many options in between the two polarized viewpoints.

I know my views of work and motherhood have changed dramatically in my short life span. In college I intended my life to be highly career minded, putting career first and waiting to get married, and perhaps never having any children. All that changed when I began to have a strong desire to have children. I experienced a change of heart. I married a year later and then five years later we had our first child. In my first year of motherhood my desire was to stay home, and I frowned on mothers who would not sacrifice for their children for these few short years. In my own mind I developed a hierarchy of moms. Those moms who stayed at home were at the top, followed by those who volunteered part-time. Next were those who worked part-time and at the bottom of my list came those who worked full-time.

After a year or two of staying home and feeling frustrated and unfulfilled and not knowing exactly why, I reexamined myself and reexamined the issue of work. My examination included a rereading of my GLC Profile. I asked myself, "Who am I as a person and how do I make this fit into being a mother?" I had been taking the job description of being a mother and trying to make myself fit into it. You know an at-home mom should be like _____. Perhaps you've done this to yourself. It's really not a healthy way to think. Now I look at myself and the job of motherhood and try to alter the job to fit the person I am. Therefore, I am less concerned with the shoulds, oughts, and extremes of either the feminist mind-set or the traditionalist mind-set.

I also examined my values. I felt a tug to work exclusively at home so that I could devote most of my energy to my children. Then I would be able to train them up in the way they should go and love them and enjoy them.

Yet I also had a strong desire to work for pay. I went directly to the source of my values, the Bible, to find out what God had to say about this issue. In Proverbs I read the description of an excellent wife: "She considers a field and buys it. From her earnings she plants a vineyard. . . . She makes linen garments and sells them, and supplies belts to the tradesmen" (Proverbs 31:16, 24, NASB). Though she manages her home well, she also works for pay. Working for pay would not be going against my values. How refreshing that this woman written about over 2,000 years ago was described as an excellent wife because of her work in and out of her home!

Now my hierarchy has changed. The women I admire the most do not fit either the traditionalist pattern or the feminist pattern; rather, they make motherhood work for themselves and their families. I don't care if that means working at home for no pay, having a home-based business, volunteering time to a worthy cause, or working outside of the home. My thinking has changed to reflect the Green Light Concept.

Middle Ground

Fortunately there is a middle ground where we don't have to choose one or the other, feminism or traditionalism. I like the counsel of Dr. Pierre Mornell, who said that "the answer begins with a woman's trying to recognize her own basic complexities and contradictory feelings. . . . A woman should be able to be both independent and dependent, active and passive, relaxed and serious, practical and romantic, tender and tough-minded, thinking and feeling, dominant and submissive."[2] Many of us don't want to devote all of our energies to our kids, husband, and house. But neither do we want to spend all of our energies on a high-powered career. This doesn't make us wishy-washy. It makes us compassionate. It makes us sensitive. It makes us multifaceted. In a word, it makes us women.

Three Questions

Reasonable adults can see the pluses and the minuses to both sides. Because the issues are complex, there are a number of considerations to the mommy wars debate. But for the sake of simplicity and understanding, a mother can sort out her role by considering three basic issues.

When Should You Go Back to Work?

How old should a child be when the mother works? Once the youngest child enters first grade the big debate virtually ends. The preschool years are called the formative years. There are experts who can tell you exactly what you want to hear. Some experts insist that the child needs the mother most of the time during the first six years. Others experts say that it makes no difference who watches your child as long as the caregiver is fair and loving. In your own heart you need to examine what is best for your kids.

How Much Say Should Your Peers Have?

How much influence should your peer group or peer groups have on your decision whether to work for pay? Many feminists would have all women working for pay, while many traditionalists would have all women working at home. There are many options in between the two of these polar viewpoints (discussed in the next chapter). Consider the peer groups that you have and consider the influences and expectations that these groups exert in your life. For example, I attend a church where many of the moms work full-time at home or part-time for pay. The expectation is that I will also work at home or part-time for pay. Another peer group for me is my neighborhood. Again many moms work at home full-time. Another peer group is my circle of friends. There is quite a mix here. It is divided between work part-time and work at home, with some women who work full-time. Peer groups for you may include coworkers or former coworkers, college friends, family members and husband's coworkers.

What Is Your Uniqueness?

No one is made like you. No one knows you better than you. Even though the women's movements of the sixties, seventies, and eighties changed much, a society and its trends cannot decide for you. Perhaps the forerunner women in these movements once believed they battled for all women. Maybe they believed that if they prevailed, the natural choice would be that a woman would no longer need to struggle with the issue of work. That's not the case. Each woman engages in her own private battle with herself. She wrestles over the issues and makes this tough decision alone.

And we change our minds about this decision as we change or our values change or our circumstances change. No matter how much you plan and anticipate, your decision may be very different when you actually have a child or two. Like me, before kids, you may have thought you would work at home with the kids but changed your mind afterwards. Or you could have thought you needed to go to work before kids, but then you held your precious baby and could not bear the thought of returning to work until that baby went to school. That's why I'll retain the image of the *thirty-something* mother, Hope Stedman, in my mind for a long time as she faced a room full of accusers. She faced them alone, which is what we all do with the ghosts that haunt us over working for pay or working at home. Mostly, I like the image of her holding onto her daughter's doll. The doll symbolizes her children. When she faced her accusers about working or not, she had in mind her children when she made that all important decision.

Status Hierarchy

Our lives cannot be lived apart from the influence and values of the society that we live in. Many of us have been born and raised in this country. Now it is our turn to birth and raise our children here. But how do we feel about living in a society where the card manufacturers, the florists, and the candy makers profit from the annual rite of Mother's Day? By the end of the week the card has been destroyed by children, the flowers have wilted, and the chocolate has been devoured. And we, as moms, are left to deal with society's view of moms for another 51 weeks. Motherhood is not all mistiness and sleeping and cooing babies, as portrayed by the cards. It is sometimes. But a lot of the time it's work.

In our society there are not enough serious books about the job of mothering, the importance of motherhood in raising the next generation, or about meeting the needs of the mother. If you browse through a bookstore, you cannot miss the large number of managerial and professional books. It seems that the needs of all professional, paid workers are met. Lest you think I am being sexist, I assure you that prestige is based on occupation rather than the worker's sex. Who gets more respect, a man who is a nurse or a man who is a doctor?

The highly rated jobs are the ones that hold authority, such as manager or supervisor. Next come the professional people with a degree. Still later come the manual laborers. And somewhere around the bottom of the ranking come homemaker and mother.

Have we faced the reality that our society influences us more than we like to admit? I think of the phrase from the Bible, "Don't let the world around you squeeze you into its own mould" (Romans 12:2, PHILLIPS). I need to get a firm grasp on the truth of this statement when I consider what is best for myself and my family. I need to disregard the movements and fluctuations of a fickle society.

When will we realize that all work is work? And that the value of work need not be based on perceived prestige? All work redeems itself when done with proper motives, when it is not illegal or immoral, and when it is done to the best of one's ability. I often hear that there should be equal pay for equal work. I believe there should be equal respect for differing, yet just as valuable, work.

Earning Hierarchy

And speaking of equal pay, we need to consider the aspect of finances in our society and how that relates to our urge for work. Hot fudge on vanilla ice cream is similar to status and earning. Status and earning are very interrelated, yet need to be discussed separately. The person who earns the most money is at the top of the pile in our society. He or she is emulated, mimicked, and admired, almost without regard for the person's character. We look past the shortcomings because we love the aura of money. Lower-paying jobs command less respect. People unable to find steady and well-paying work are looked down on as lazy or somehow inadequate. Somewhere near the bottom of the pile are the mothers who have no earnings of their own, even though they do a lot of work.

Am I exaggerating the importance of money? Let me answer this way: Do you ever wish that you could have a job just so that you can have a paycheck of your own— your own money? I know I do and I know other women who do too. Money has its own allure.

Consider the not-too-subtle ways society devalues the woman who chooses to work at home for no pay:

> ◆ The Internal Revenue Service calls a spouse who works at home caring for children for no pay—which is what most stay-at-home moms are—a *nonworking spouse*. The so-called *nonworking spouse* is granted a mere $250 deduction toward an Individual Retirement Account (IRA). The "working" spouse is entitled to a full $2000 IRA deduction (if he or she earns at least $2000 that year). Additionally, the IRS does not allow a so-called nonworking spouse to deduct child care costs incurred for pursuing a hobby, doing volunteer activities, or getting time away from the children— only for work that produces income.[3]

> ◆ Consider the economics of being at home with your children. From the magazine *Working Mother*, "The latest figures for the median weekly earnings of a family in which both partners work is $859. If only Dad works, weekly earnings are $506. If Mom is the only breadwinner, family income is $347 a week."[4]

In effect, the woman who works at home caring for children is hit with a triple whammy:

♦ Her family's income is low in comparison to others, giving her less money with which to support a family.

♦ She is not allowed to take deductions for child care and only extremely limited deductions for an IRA.

♦ Her tax dollars, in effect, are used to subsidize daycare for moms who work for pay—whose families, on the average, make more than hers.

I don't think I am making too much of the money issue. Consider the popular saying on T-shirts and bumper stickers: "He who dies with the most toys wins." It would be humorous except that our furious pace of buying shows that we do want the most toys and the best toys. VCR's, TV's, and cars become outdated quickly as manufacturers add new bells and whistles, new buttons, and gizmos and gadgets. And we buy. And the bumper sticker pales in comparison with the truth that "We brought nothing with us when we entered this world and we can be sure we shall take nothing with us when we leave it."[5]

Who Chooses for Whom?

Should we sigh and resign ourselves to the influences of society? Should we feel helpless and (worse still) hopeless about pursuing our lifetime dreams? May it not be the case for you or for me.

We must realize that we have a choice. Oftentimes I've heard moms who work for pay say, "I've just got to work. We need the money." Similarly, I've talked with women who work at home who say they feel they must stay home with the children during their formative years. Again, we must realize that we have a choice.

How Do We Choose?

If we can get beyond the expectations of peer groups or just society in general, we can stop being so defensive or guilty about the work decisions we have made by using what I call the Family Equation. We have a column in our local paper called "How's the Family Doing?" The GLC Family Equation reminds me of that column. Basically, the Family Equation asks: "With all of our activities, commitments and responsibilities how is the family doing?"

You've got to understand my engineering background a little to understand the equation concept. I like to contemplate systems and come up with a neat, tidy little formula or an explanation for everything. The family equation would be: a husband's time spent working for pay plus her time spent working for pay, multiplied by their time spent with the kids, divided by the time they spend on household chores, squared, plus the sum of the fulfillment levels of each family member. Well, that's all wrong. I cannot come up with an equation for your family that works for you, just as you cannot develop an equation for my family that works for us. Each family's equation will be unique to them. But one of the big questions is, "Is this (situation) working for all of us as individuals and as a family?" You'll have to forge out your own family equation. In our family we put all the variables on the table and examine all of our options, needs, and desires when forming our own Family Equation.

Our Family Equation has a lot to do with the Greens that I, my husband, and our children want to pursue. Dave is in a very technical engineering position to use his Green. He also writes computer programs in his off hours to use his Green further. But he agrees that I need to work beyond the work that I do with the kids and in the house; I don't get enough fulfillment from mothering alone. By doing my Green—reading, writing, and researching—anywhere from five to twenty-five hours a week, I maintain my sense of balance.

Fluctuations in our Family Equation depend on kids' schedules, sicknesses, and other obligations. When I'm hot on writing or have a deadline, my husband takes the kids more often and longer that week. When he is hot on something he is working on, the kids are mine. The trouble occurs when we both want to work at the same time. At those times we hire a baby-sitter or we fight about who gets the children. Three afternoons a week I hire a baby-sitter for Nathan while Hannah is at preschool. Then I have concentrated, uninterrupted time to write—usually.

Nathan's "Green" is anything to do with balls, rough-housing, and climbing. Once a week he goes to Wee Play where he does those things. And I've even sacrificed my nice respectable-looking kitchen to hang up a basketball hoop on the refrigerator for him.

Hannah loves art and dance. She does art at school. Also, at home we have a permanent place for her to do art anytime she wants. She attends dance lessons once a week. And then there are times that she plays with neighborhood kids.

Other activities that we are involved in include time with friends, time spent on maintaining our house, and time spent going to church. We have family times together and also get to know, as a family, some international college students. Just for me is my mother's support group, for help and encouragement in being a mom. It works for us—people's needs are being met.

Does scheduling all this work out perfectly for us? With two kids and two careers and volunteer activities and an old house, no, not at all. Something is usually going haywire. But we do have a framework with which to work. And sometimes we don't have bread for peanut butter and jelly (our lunch staple), milk for morning cereal, or diapers for Nathan. With such a schedule, some activities aren't done very often or done very well. Laundry is not done very often, but thanks to the makers of Stain Stick I can goop up my kids' clothes and wash them up to a week later. Our house is never spotless, but it's usually clean. I like to cook some foods but others, such as spaghetti sauce, I buy ready-made. But as I spend time in my Greens and steal it away from other things, I have time for kids, for myself, and for my husband— three big parts of my life. And my husband prefers a happy wife with a messy house to a perfectly run household with a neurotic, frustrated, complaining wife.

Factors in Your Family Equation

What works for you and your family? How's your family going to consider all of the priorities competing for your time? Let's look at six factors that affect every Family Equation.

Everyone Needs Greens

The first factor you need to consider in working out your Family Equation is that all family members need to use their GLC Profile and to develop their Green Action Skills. In the case of children, this means giving them exposure to different activities and the opportunity to discover their Greens. For both husband and wife, this means pursuing jobs or activities they love.

For the short-term a person can ignore his or her Greens and be OK. But over the long haul a person will become irritable and not a pleasant person to be around. I need to use my Greens consistently; otherwise I am an awful person to be around. I'm not a big fan of the philosophy that a woman can and should tough it out and sacrifice while the children are little. Sometimes I've been told a woman should do this because her kids are only young for a short time. Let me tell you, five to ten years is not short when you don't like very much of your job. Men are encouraged to be fulfilled in their jobs and vocations (though few men are); why should a wife be expected to tough it out when a husband is expected to pursue a job he loves? A caring husband wants to see his wife obtain some sense of fulfillment and accomplishment, regardless of the ages of the children. A mom especially needs encouragement since she tends to be the primary one trying to meet other family members' needs.

What Your Husband Wants

The second factor is the issue of when a wife's desire to work conflicts with her husband's desire for her not to work. How does your husband feel about you working? Does he agree that you need work beyond the house and the children? How will he adjust to your additional commitments? Will he lower his expectations of how much housework you can do? Will he watch the children while you pursue your Greens?

My husband has rolled with the punches ever since I took on paying work. But sometimes he is annoyed that some chores are not done anymore or are done less frequently. As an example, he recently longed for home-made spaghetti sauce, which I used to make for him. I tried to talk him out of it by saying that the canned sauce was pretty good and costs about the same, on sale, as making my own. Still he wouldn't budge. Finally, I said, "I don't have time to make homemade sauce; I'm trying to finish writing this book." He decided that it was worth his own time to make a batch. And knowing that it was worth his time makes me want to do it for him (after the book is finished, of course).

The Well-being of the Children

The third factor is the well-being of the children. Before I had kids, I once got counsel that I should work for my own benefit. Wisely, that counselor added, "Make sure, though, that you put the needs of your kids first." Certainly, holding a child in her arms changes a woman's perspective. Women who have thought they'd return to work have changed their minds as they've held their baby.

Part-time work is one solution to this dilemma. Sometimes it comes down to the choice of full-time work or no paid work. Then a mom has a tough decision to make about who to put first, herself or her kids. The question I ask is, "Do I spend unhurried time alone with them on a daily basis, and do they know that they can interrupt me at any time because I love them and because they come before my paid work?"

Your Season of Life

The fourth factor to consider is the season of life you are in. Have you evaluated your life and adjusted your commitments according to your present circumstances?

One of the most stretching times of life is that of early parenthood. The children require a lot of time and care, careers scream for attention, and financial pressures squeeze from all sides. The Family Equation in our household changes constantly. It fluctuates with the small mini-crises of too many sleepless nights in a row, sicknesses, overtime work for my husband, and deadlines for me. Times of bigger changes, such as a job layoff, adding a new baby, moving to a new house, and a child starting school can further disrupt the equilibrium. Therefore, figuring out the Family Equation is not a one-time decision; it's a dynamic decision-making process. What is needed is periodic evaluation and adjustment throughout life because life is full of changes. And as a mom your season in life revolves around the ages and activities of your children.

The next stage, when the children are in elementary school, is generally an easier stage. After that, the season of teenage parenthood, is, I've been told, like a full-blown version of the Terrible Twos. Realize the seasons in your life and be kind to yourself through each one.

Everyone's Energy Level

A fifth factor in your Family Equation is everyone's individual energy level. You have to consider what energy level you all have and allocate your time wisely. If I am trying to do more than I have energy for, I feel as though I'm shortchanging everyone and not doing a good job at anything. When I feel frazzled and worn-out, I ease up on some of my responsibilities. I am not a high-energy person. Also, you need to consider whether there are any situations in your life that give you less time and energy than a typical family needs, such as a family member with a permanent illness or disability, a parent with Alzheimer's, or an aging parent who needs lots of care.

What You Are Willing to Give Up

The sixth factor is the reality that you will always need to give up something when you say yes to something else. In my case, I have chosen to forfeit some time with my kids, some time spent cleaning my house, and some time with friends in order to pursue my lifetime dream of writing. Some people give up money in order to hire help to clean the house or make meals for the family. Some moms give up the opportunity to make money in order to be with their children. Each mom needs to evaluate what she is willing to give up for the sake of pursuing something else. The freedom of choice does not come without a cost.

And with this freedom, the right of complaining vanishes. Once you have chosen a lifestyle, you are not free to complain about the choice you've made. And you are not free to look at others and complain about their lifestyle either. Life is a series of choices, and with each comes some cost and benefits for which you have to take responsibility. Each choice you make is just that—*your* choice.

Values

Intricately woven into your choices and the factors in the Family Equation are your family values. What do you, as a family, base your decisions on? Each family has a pattern or a means of evaluating their lifestyle choices. Sometimes it isn't clear how a particular family makes decisions, but underlying the outward behavior is a reason why. Our family has chosen the Bible, believing its words are from God for our benefit.

We've learned from the Bible that God is pleased when we help others. Thus, many of our lifetime dreams involve helping people. In our family relationships, we choose to love, to spend time with one another, and to serve one another, even though relationships are a Red for both me and my husband. Despite the fact that many of the homemaking jobs are Reds for me, I choose to be a good manager of my home in order to be the kind of wife God wants me to be.

Frankly, the Green Light Concept is not just about discovering your Greens and using them; it is about setting realistic expectations. It is about creating harmonious family relationships. And it is also about making sure that each member of the family is able to use his or her strengths and areas of competence. The Green Light Concept takes into consideration all of life in the decision-making process: choices, values, responsibilities, and setting a lifestyle. That may be tough to implement, but then life has no easy answers.

The Rest of Your Life

I have a fondness for Hope, the mother in the *thirtysomething* series. Our children are approximately the same ages and I find myself identifying with Hope in her struggles to carve out a Family Equation and yet still use her Greens in writing. Her struggles are very familiar to me. I like Hope because she has real struggles; she changes her mind and life changes her.

What was Hope's answer to the question of what to do with the rest of her life? With resolve and courage, Hope said, "I still don't know." What refreshing honesty. I wish I could say the pressures never bothered Hope again. I wish I could say that she lived happily ever after. All I can say is that she chose to live her own life by shrugging off peer pressure this time and by living her life as she decided best for her and her family.[6]

More importantly, what will you do with the rest of your life? What—you don't even know what you're having for dinner? Me either. Oh well. Many moms don't know what they want the future to hold. But I encourage you to try to figure it out.

The next chapter deals with options for moms. These options can help you further pursue your lifetime dream, or they may clarify why your dream may have to remain on the back burner for now. It's OK not to have all of life figured out and planned. It's OK to change your mind. It's not OK to ignore who you are.

Chapter 10

What's a Mother to Do?

◆

"No workie, no eatie." I can still hear my grandfather saying it as we raked leaves in the fall. We kids knew that if we didn't finish raking, we wouldn't get to have cookies and milk with grandpa. He was a man of his word. That was over twenty years ago. Today I still agree with my grandfather—everyone needs to work, and everyone needs significant work. I tell my kids, "Everyone has work. Mommy's job is to take care of you two, clean the house, cook, and write. Your job is to take care of your toys, help each other, clean your rooms, and brush your teeth."

I think that's why the question "Oh, do you work?" insults me. You bet I work, and I say so! A person's response is usually the platitude, "You know—I meant for money." Money has distorted the value of work.

So rather than discuss work options based on money,

I will draw my lines on the attitude of work and the time spent pursuing work. After all, the saying, "All mothers are working mothers" is true. The categories of work are Homemaker, Full-timer, and Adapter. Please know that with time, many women experience all of these categories. You have the freedom to move among them.

Homemaker is the woman who considers homemaking her most important job. She has made a value judgment to put the needs of her children, her husband, and her home first, sometimes to the point of ignoring her own needs.

Full-timer is the woman who works for pay full-time outside of her home. For any number of the following reasons, she wants to or has to work: she has made a value judgment that her career goals are a high priority in her life; she is a single mom with no other means to support her family; she feels that her career would suffer if she worked for pay any less than full-time; she was unable to find part-time work, though she pursued that option; she has developed a lifestyle that requires a certain amount of money; her family needs the income for survival.

Adapter tries to meet the needs of her family without neglecting her own needs. Thus, she finds ways to work for pay part-time, in a home-based business, or in a volunteer capacity. She has one foot solidly in each of the two camps of Homemaker and Full-timer. She is usually best able to understand the polar viewpoints of both groups of women. Adapters have been known to do the following: paid part-time work outside of the home; paid part-time work at home; paid part-time sales/demonstration work; work for herself as an entrepreneur; work as a free-lancer; work at seasonal or temporary jobs; volunteer for activities outside the house that do not revolve around the children; pursuing education to prepare for paid work later.

The rest of this chapter examines a little more what being a Homemaker, Full-timer, and Adapter involves (sometimes it isn't a pretty sight). I'll consider the advantages and disadvantages of each choice. The categories themselves are just a handle; they aren't meant to box you in. I myself have gone from Full-timer to Homemaker to Adapter. And I'm not sure what changes the future will bring.

Homemaker

If you are a Homemaker, you know the benefits of working at home: quality, unrushed time with your children. You have time for housework and errands. You have time to get together with other women and friends.

But there are also pitfalls. While doing research at the library last year I used the *Reader's Guide to Periodical Literature*. I looked under "women" and found many subcategories, but something was missing. I thought there must have been a mistake, or that I missed it. So I looked again at the listings under women; I read, "Accountants, Air pilots, Anthropologists, Architects, Artists, Astronauts, Astronomers, Athletes, Authors, Auto drivers, Bankers, Baseball umpires, Basketball coaches, Biologists, Bishops, Body builders, Brokers," and on through the C's until the end of the alphabet. There was no category for women as homemakers, women as caregivers, or women as mothers. The percentage of women in the United States who have children no doubt exceeds the percentage of women umpires in the United States. What does this say about motherhood as a serious profession? Was I no longer a woman because I was a mom?

Pitfall One: No Respect

I belabor this point because women who choose to work at home full-time are in for a battle—a battle of not being taken seriously by society or by women working for pay (whether full-time or part-time). Let's call this pitfall number one. A Homemaker needs to be sure of her decision for her own sense of well-being. Our society is not going to encourage her. Also, because she is in a vulnerable position of working at meeting others' needs, her own needs might not be met. Since working at home with the children is a value judgment, she has given herself no option to pursue work outside the home.

Pitfall Two: Financial Crunch

Pitfall number two is the financial restraints. You do not earn money, so you have to make one paycheck cover everything. You may spend more time economizing by baking from scratch, making your own curtains, painting rather than wallpapering, decorating frugally, and shopping the sales. As a Homemaker, you may have to sacrifice some material goals. You may have to live in a two family house instead of a single family unit, or maybe not afford a house at all. You may have to get by with one car instead of two, or maybe two well-used used cars. Instead of vacationing in Disney World, you may have to scale down vacations to a nearby cottage rental or something less expensive, like camping—or perhaps not even taking a vacation at all. You may have to use more hand-me-down clothes and buy fewer clothes for yourself (usually this seems to be the case).

If you are a Homemaker, I'm sure you have other money saving ideas. I applaud women who choose to make sacrifices to spend time with their children. Your efforts are not unimportant, they are not unnoticed, and, most important, you are not alone.

Do the financial restraints of being a Homemaker give you a right to complain? It is unbecoming to complain if it is a choice that you and your husband have made. I've caught myself doing it, and it's not right. If you've chosen to be a homemaker, you've made a choice; do not complain and grumble as you live out that choice. There is a price to be paid for every decision. The decision to be a homemaker usually means that a family has less money to live on than other families. But that is the price for working at home and giving your kids yourself. In the June and July 1990 *Parents Magazine*, 94 percent of work at home moms said being at home with their kids was the number one reason they stayed at home.[1]

Pitfall Three: Dependency

Pitfall number three is the dependency on your husband that you may develop. There is no doubt that a mom with preschool children who chooses to work at home is in a most vulnerable position financially and emotionally. In the case of a divorce, it would be difficult for you to return to work and support your family. Also, in the daily routine now, you have probably developed dependency on your husband. In effect, he may have become your supervisor; your boss. You look to him for encouragement and approval because your world is the home, your husband, and the kids. This is what happened when I was working at home full-time.

However, my husband's GLC Profile is such that supervision is a Red for him. He was at a loss as to how to encourage me; he'd start to set up regular evaluations for me, but within a short time he stopped. Just as in the real world, I wanted feedback and encouragement for the work I was doing at home. I wanted promotions, job evaluations, and perks, as in the outside world of work. My frustration grew as I expected this more from him and wasn't getting positive supervision. He couldn't understand that I needed encouragement. After kids, my whole world changed, while he continued to work a forty hour a week job and receive the benefits of pay, a supervisor, a yearly review, people telling him he was doing a good job, and the support of his coworkers. Certainly his life at home changed—and not for the better, I might add.

If your husband, like mine, is not a natural supervisor, then he can make a commitment to supervise you (apart from your coaching him to do so), knowing that it is his Red; just realize that he will do a fair to poor job of it. In any event, I encourage you to accept your husband's design.

But if your husband is a supervisor, his oversight will help you. A positive supervisor knows his workers—in this case, you—well. He knows your Greens, Yellows, and Reds. He evaluates your performance based on who you are. For example, if your Green is Ideas and your Red is Tasks, then you will spend more time sewing and creating than cleaning and organizing. He will take this into account when he gives you feedback. He will encourage you to spend time doing your Greens and love you through your Reds.

To help avoid becoming too dependent on your husband, you need a support system. You need more than your husband and your kids. A support system could be any one or more of the following: an organized group of women who meet regularly to help and encourage one another; a group of friends; or a best friend with whom you talk daily. You need someone who can help you with the frustrations of motherhood. I suggest that you get one other person in similar circumstances who knows you intimately. It would be good to find a woman with children who are the same approximate ages as your children. Find someone who knows the ins and outs of raising children and maintaining a household and meeting a woman's needs. Find someone who you can bounce ideas off of and someone who'll give you feedback.

Relationships people need more positive supervision than any other GLC Profile. Without positive encouragement, they are crushed easily. Still other women with different strengths, particularly Tasks and Strategy people, prefer to have little or no supervision. Ideas people need a moderate amount of supervision.

Full-timer

Like Homemaker, Full-timer has her own set of advantages. Money earned is a help to the family in these economic times. She can feel good about working. Possibly she has work utilizing her Greens more than if she worked at home. If so, then she feels better about herself because she works, and that may help her frame of mind while mothering. Yet if she works because of economic necessity, she may resent her job and the time it takes away from her family time. She is less dependent on her husband; they have more of an egalitarian relationship. Because she works, her career advancement does not suffer.

Pitfall One: A Hurried Pace

However, this choice has its pitfalls too. First, after work responsibilities, home, husband, and kids, there is little free time left over. It is difficult to do even basic errand-running. The dinner hour may tend toward hurried chaos, or may not even exist. She may feel pulled in many directions during her off work hours meeting the needs of kids, house, and husband. Being a Full-timer leaves little time for herself or time with friends.

The Full-timers I know overcome this pitfall by being very organized. These women have developed systems for housecleaning, shopping, cooking, and getting everybody out the door in the morning. A lot of activities are

fairly strictly scheduled. And every thing and posses-
sion has a place. Full-timers have to be organized to
avoid total chaos.

This lifestyle is particularly good for Tasks women,
as they enjoy systems and schedules. Strategy women
enjoy the busyness of it all. Relationships and Ideas
women dislike this lifestyle generally because the systems and schedules are Reds for them, and because the
busyness takes time away from people.

If you are a Full-timer, because you have so little time
in which to get so much done, it may be necessary for
you to concentrate your lifestyle and eliminate some
responsibilities. You could hire a house cleaner and rely
more on fast foods or prepared foods. Extra money could
buy you some much needed extra time. In your case,
time is money. As you pay for services, you will have
more time for your kids.

But before you spend freely to make up for lost time,
do a cost analysis to make sure you are not squandering
the gain your employment brings. Subtract from your
take-home pay the following expenses:

- ♦ Child care
- ♦ Fast food
- ♦ Housecleaning
- ♦ Work clothes
- ♦ Transportation
- ♦ Miscellaneous and other work-related
  expenses

Certainly money is not the only reason you work. But
if the financial benefit is all but wiped out by the expenses
of your employment, perhaps some other alternative is
worth consideration.

Pitfall Two: Less Time with Your Children

The second pitfall is having less time with your children. If your children are under the age of six, your peer groups may expect you to limit your work-for-pay hours. You may feel pressure to defend your choice or feel guilty about it, though after the children enter school full time this lessens for many women.

Concerning the issue of guilt, I found an article in *Parents Magazine*, July 1991. In the article "Feeling Guilty" by Leslie Bennetts, she quotes from Antoinette Saunders, "If you're feeling guilty about not spending enough time with your kids, maybe you need to figure out ways to spend more time with them. A lot of decisions we make are often not in the best interests of our kids." Not all guilt is bad. Some helps us to make changes that benefit our family. The article mentions foregoing an exercise program or a lot of nights out to avoid spending too much time away from the kids. In the end, only you can decide how much of your non-work time you will spend with your children. I encourage you to spend as much of it as you can with them, as Saunders suggests.

There are some other ways to make more time for your kids. You could approach your boss with a proposal to work afternoons and evenings so that you can have mornings with the kids. You could ask your boss to consider allowing you to work some of your hours at home. If you can work part-time during July and August, you can spend more time with your kids during the summer. While at work, concentrate on making a support friend of at least one coworker so you can have nights freed up for time with the children. Better yet, walk briskly during lunch time as you talk with this friend so that your exercise requirement is also fulfilled. Realize that by working you are meeting *your* needs, and cut back on other activities that are "just for you."

Since you spend so much time working, it would be wise to have a job that is solidly in your Green Focus area. Otherwise, your job will be a constant drain on you. The combination of a mismatched job with the possible guilt from not being with your children for a significant part of most days will leave you frustrated and emotionally exhausted, with little time or energy for your children, yourself, or your spouse. In contrast, having a job in your Green will tend to energize rather than drain you.

Adapter

Somewhere in between Homemaker and Full-timer is a more moderate, more balanced pace of life and living. Though still not easy, it is a compromise between the two extremes of Homemaker and Full-timer. It can be the best of both worlds: You have time with your kids, time for some housework, time for your husband, and time for fulfilling work beyond the home.

The Pitfalls: Compromise

At times it can also be the worst of both worlds. As a part-time worker, you are generally not respected as much as a Full-timer. Your paycheck is sometimes called "extra money," as if you didn't need it (or are spoiled by having it). Some others may view your paid work as a diversion, hobby, or as simply a break from the kids. Job promotions for part-timers are rarely as generous as for Full-timers. You may feel guilty for not spending enough time with your kids. And sometimes, or often, you may feel stretched.

Lately I've known the "stretched feeling" a lot. As I come to the homestretch of writing this manuscript, I find myself creeping more and more into a full-time role. Fifteen hours a week the kids are with a paid sitter, and I sneak in two hours a night after they go to bed and another hour before they wake up. My husband watches them three or four evenings a week. They show signs of needing me more, but so does this book. I am beginning to feel guilty about lack of time with them. I tell myself that it will only be temporary. Still, for the past couple of months I have made this book a priority over my kids. And I am enjoying it.

I believe that most women would say they are Adapters at heart. In talking to women I know, part-time work seems to be their preferred choice. It allows them substantial time to be with their children. It enables them to keep their brains from becoming Cream of Wheat. Part-time paid work brings in money to help the family financially. It gives them some healthy independence and esteem. And it often gives them more opportunities to use their Green Action Skills, outside of the home environment.

If You Could Do Whatever You Wanted...

The *Ladies Home Journal* conducted a mail-in survey entitled, "The American Mother: A Landmark Survey for the 1990's." About 22,000 women mailed in responses. Coming as no surprise to us moms was that "eighty percent of employed women wish they had the luxury of working part-time." Surprisingly, "71 percent said they're pleased with the child-care arrangements they've chosen."[2]

And in another survey appearing in *Parents Magazine*, women responded to a questionnaire asking about women and work. One question in particular struck me: "If you could do whatever you wanted, what would you do?" Here are the results:

62% would work part-time

25% would stay at home full time (work at home for no pay)

8% would work full-time

And this is how these women actually live:

28% work part-time

34% stay at home

39% work full-time

An awful lot of moms who now work full-time want to work part-time. Some moms who are now working at home for no pay want to work part-time.[3]

My interpretation of these surveys is that women generally do not want to put their careers ahead of their children. For the most part, mothers are moderates, seeking neither the role of Homemaker nor Full-timer. Women with children do not want one or the other—a career or time with the kids. Rather, they tend to say, "I am no good seeing my children too little, and I am no good being around them too much."[4] This statement encapsulates the part-time craving of today's moms who want the best of both worlds. The majority would work part-time if they could.

If part-time is the choice of preference, than why don't more moms choose it? There are a number of reasons. Some don't exercise the option because of decreased pay or benefits relative to full-time work. Many moms dislike the so-called "mommy track" because of the fear of falling behind in their field. In our society there is still the attitude that a part-time worker is not as professional and not as dedicated as her full-time counterparts (though the studies I've seen show the opposite—part-timers are dedicated to their work and get more done in their part-time hours than the full-timers get done in the same time period). The availability of part-time jobs is certainly a problem; many times good part-time work is not available. (Women don't just want to work, they want to work at something they enjoy doing.) Companies sometimes take advantage of women with children who want to work part-time, whom they can pay less and deny key benefits. I agree with Tony Campolo, who wrote, "Employers are well aware that women who are desperate to work part time in order to be available for their children are easy to exploit, and they quite frequently take advantage of these women."[5] My own search for part-time work was frustrating. For each of the positions I applied for, the personnel offices received many more applicants than they expected.

Some great achieving women spent their early motherhood years as part-timers. Later they rose in their fields to become the cream of the crop. For example, Jeanne Kirkpatrick raised three children before attaining the status of United Nations Ambassador for the U.S. I admired her a lot before I knew she was a wife and a mother, but now I really admire her for the time she "laid low" for the good of her family. She didn't let all her lifetime dreams go either, but put them on the back burner until a more appropriate time.[6]

Trish had Emily for one year before she felt being at home all the time just wasn't in her personality. She missed going out as an adult, getting dressed up, being stimulated by adult conversation, and earning money. She was able to find a part-time job three mornings a week working for a lawyer. Still she is able to give her daughter time. She has time for her house, errands, entertaining, friends, and volunteering. Trish feels better about herself because she works and she thinks that reflects in the good job she does with Emily during her (non-paid) working hours at home. She has another source of fulfillment besides her house, husband, and child.

Karen knew that she wanted to spend significant amounts of time with her newborn daughter while leaving room for volunteering. Yet she wanted to earn money, too. She decided to sew fabric flags from her home, sometimes with baby underfoot, sometimes while baby napped, sometimes while husband watched baby, and sometimes late at night while baby slept. She's done this sewing for years, steadily and consistently. Since then her baby has grown into a young lady, and she's added a new baby.

Jean was tired of being a Full-timer because she was missing out on seeing her children grow up. She lamented to me that I was lucky to be able to stay home with my kids. (I thought it wasn't luck but a matter of choices I'd made.) After baby number two, she approached her company with the proposition of working half-time. Her request was denied; she could either work full-time or not at all. Jean had a tough choice to make, but she made it—she decided to pursue sales and demonstration work. She now works half-time as a manager and demonstrator, and she's happy with her choice. At night her husband cares for the children. During the day her mother or grandmother is able to watch the kids when Jean can't. She spends more time with her kids, which is what Jean wanted, while not having to give up out-of-home work altogether. This situation fits in with Jean's family equation. Her family is doing fine.

Tricia worked as an editor before the birth of her first child. She now has two girls. She solved the work dilemma by freelancing her skills and talents as an editor. She receives an assignment to work on, completes it at home, and mails it to her employer. She may not remember, but Tricia once said casually while using her Greens to organize and alphabetize a pile of name tags: "I can be obsessed with other things besides my kids. I'm happier, my kids are happier, and my husband is happier too." Isn't that wonderful to hear?

Entrepreneur Adapters

Some Adapters have entrepreneurial tendencies. I place myself more in this category than in any other. I have the flexibility to work or not as opportunities arise. I have time to do volunteer work, to spend a lot of time with my kids, and to choose my work topics and my work hours. My biggest disadvantage is never knowing how much money I will earn. For now that is my choice. And thus far it's worked out (for the most part) because my husband earns a good salary and we have designed a lifestyle (a two-family house that we repair ourselves) that enables us to live on one salary. But as the children enter school and our longing for a single family home increases, we will need to make some decisions.

Seasonal-, Temporary-, and Substitute-adapters

Still other moms choose to work only during certain times of the year. Sue works part-time during the school year at her children's school as a teacher's aide. She earns enough to make it worth her while, and she enjoys the work. A woman I used to know prepared tax returns during February, March, and April, earning money and putting her accounting degree to work. Still other moms work for pay only during the holiday season. Others go on call for substitute teaching or temporary work.

Volunteer Adapters

I credit George and Barbara Bush with elevating the status of volunteers in this country. I always knew what

George meant by "A thousand points of light." And Barbara, by her example, has shown us the value and worth of volunteerism. Barbara Bush has spent most of her life raising her family, and did a little more. At the time she handled motherhood by "listening to George's reassurances that what she'd always done was important." But as her children left, she threw "herself into volunteer work."[7] The amount of money in the form of time donated per year is a significant contribution to our society. In coming years there will be less money to spend on social programs because of the national debt and the unbalanced United States budget. Volunteers can fill these very real gaps and can make an impact in the lives of people. Volunteering can also lead to job opportunities later, especially if you've used your Green and Yellow Focus areas in your volunteer jobs.

Having something beyond yourself and your family to devote significant amounts of time to requires the same juggling and persistence of having a part-time job, perhaps even more because you are not receiving any pay for your efforts. But if you believe in the cause you've taken up, perhaps your child's school or your church or a community project, then volunteering is for you. Just make sure you use your Greens in your volunteer responsibilities. Insist on it.

Conclusion

For most moms, regardless of the work choice they've made, the following statements are true.

- ♦ We love our children.
- ♦ We want the best for our children. Homemakers give their children the best by being there with them. Full-timers happy with their work

give their children happier moms. Adapters do both.

♦ We don't want to be boxed in by just one option. We have the freedom to move between the options. As life changes us, we need to reevaluate and rethink our options.

♦ We want to be fulfilled and happy.

♦ We envy one another. We have the tendency to complain about the choices we've made and to envy the choice others have made. On some days, Homemakers wish to work for pay. Sometimes Full-timers would love a day just with their kids. Adapters sometimes yearn for the lifestyle of a Homemaker or a Full-timer.

♦ We have doubts about our choices.

♦ We need a support group—close friends to talk to about being moms and people. No matter what kind of moms we are, we need people who love, accept, and affirm us in the job of motherhood.

As women we don't have to worry about my grandfather's saying, "No workie, no eatie." There is always plenty of work to be done. I know that the issue is a tough one. I refer you to the Family Equation discussion in Chapter Nine. Everything in your life is interrelated. Therefore, the complexity of issues is staggering. It's hard to do or to change just one thing without it affecting all aspects of your life. I hope you saw yourself somewhere in these descriptions, identifying with struggles and learning about other women's struggles. As women, we can broaden, change, and switch gears as our children grow and mature, and as we grow and mature.

For Homemaker, I suggest rereading the chapters about husband, kids, and house. My hope is that you will tailor the jobs of motherhood to fit who you are. Also, Appendix A explains more about GLC Profiles, Appendix B lists some possibilities for volunteering and hobbies, and Appendix C lists resources to encourage you in your full-time job of mothering.

If you are a Full-timer, you may wish to reread the chapters about husband, house, and kids. Also, the resources in Appendices A, B, C, and D, which offers some job hunting resources, will help you.

And if you're an Adapter, you may want to take advantage of it all, as you have one foot in both worlds.

As an aside, I was curious to find out how much the daycare issue affected the work-for-pay issue. One survey's results were published in the *Family Circle* Magazine:

What is the one thing that you feel can improve family life?

Religious values	56%
More time together	31%
Decline in divorce rate	6%
Better Law enforcement	5%
Better child care	2%

Note that child care issues were barely perceived to impact the quality of family life. The second biggest improvement could be made by spending more time together as a family. The part-time solution would give more needed family time.[8] Chapter 12 discusses the yearning for religious values in family life.

PART SIX

Maintaining Realistic Expectations by Saying No

Chapter 11

When to Say No

---◆---

"No! No! No! No!" my two-year-old shouts at the top of his lungs. For emphasis he furiously shakes his head and his upper torso with each vehement no. I tell him to look at me because his eyes have been shut and his face has been pointed at the ceiling. He looks at me. I repeat my request. Once again he repeats a series of four no's, this time slower and as a moan.

My request was simple: "Just leave the lid on the sippy cup. I'm sick of changing your entire outfit each time you have a drink." Yet Nathan's independence has arrived in a big way. He doesn't want anything that is babyish or different from the rest of the family. He is saying no honestly; no one has told him how to say no politely. He thinks no one will grant him his wishes, so his nos are emphatic.

I admire Nathan for knowing what he wants and for tenaciously pursuing it. Somewhere along the way adults forget how to say no like that. We learn to fit in with the crowd and not go against the tide, even if we desperately want to. We have become, for better or for worse, "civilized." For better because we are a functioning and contributing part of society. For worse because we often conform when we don't want to—and all because someone has asked us. For worse because we have learned to say politely, yet begrudgingly, with a learned, sincere-looking smile, "Yes," when we desperately want to scream, "No! No! No! No!"

Throughout this book I've tried to help you find solutions to relieve some of the stress that you feel as a mother, from examining the myths of the Perfect Mother to discovering your Green Focus area and relating it to many aspects of your life. I hope I've given you help in making some decisions. The decisions are all yours to make, but I would be negligent if I did not let you in on one of my biggest stress-relievers. It is the word *no*. In this chapter I'll share some practical ways you can evaluate current pressures and opportunities for possible dispatch with the word no.

Busyness

Perhaps you feel as if there are too many expectations on your time and that you are too busy. You feel like saying, "Stop the world, I want to get off for a while." Moms often have little time left after their many responsibilities. My work is never completely done. Your life may already be too full with kids and work and volunteer activities. In that case say no almost immediately to further activities.

My Time Is Finite

I don't agree with the statement, "Everybody has the same twenty-four hours a day. You just have to decide what to do with them." Not everyone has the same twenty-four hours. There is even a difference between middle-class and poor women twenty-four hours. Middle-class women, in effect, have more time because they are able to spend more of their income on occasional fast food dinners or on a baby-sitter so that they can do a house project. I have more time because I can hop in my minivan to go places, while I see other moms waiting with their little children for public transportation. Money can buy you time. Still, time is finite and choices about its use must be made.

My Energy Is Finite

Another difference in people is their personal energy levels. It makes no difference what your Green is; each person is made differently and has her own energy level. I have friends who enjoy being on the go all of the time. I feel like a dish rag if I'm as busy as they are for even a week. You need to evaluate your energy level and gauge your responsibilities with that in mind. If you are too tired, then you are not functioning at full capacity.

I Need Time with My Family

I asked a friend of mine a few months back (one who is very busy and active) if she was spending enough time with her kids. I caught her off-guard; I've never asked that question before. And apparently she'd never been asked that question before. She didn't quite know what to answer. Fumbling she said, "They're with me all the time, while I do things."

I clarified my question by saying, "Do your kids have you—your undivided attention, time when they know you're interested in just them—time when you listen, when they have you all to themselves?" Periodically, you need to evaluate whether you are making that kind of time for your children, and on a consistent basis. Maybe you have a friend who will ask you these questions. If you don't, then remember to ask yourself.

Your husband is part of the family also. Now that children have come along, your husband may be the most neglected member of the family. I know with little kids that so much of my time and energy goes into meeting their needs that, at times, I feel that I neglect my husband's needs. And too many times I really do neglect his needs. Over the long haul, he's important to me. So I want to spend good, quality, undivided-attention time with him.

I Need Time for Me

You also need "just me" time too, time when you're not working or improving yourself. "Me time" is different for each mom. You know what you need to be able to relax. I hope you can squeeze it in. Me time is when you're not pursuing your lifetime dream, not taking care of the kids, and not fulfilling other responsibilities. Activities I enjoy doing are shopping in crafty, artsy places, country shops, or antique shops. Also, I love to watch long well-made movies such as *Out of Africa* or *A Room with a View*. I like a movie that gives me a good cry or a spontaneous laugh such as *Back to the Future*. I enjoy watching a Boston Red Sox game (when they win, that is). Occasionally, I like to make a batch of cookies or to paddle on a leisurely canoe trip. But me time is not spent performing or doing—just relaxing my mind and body.

I Want and Need Time with My Friends

John Donne wrote that "No man is an Island."[1] No woman is an island either. She needs more than her husband, her kids, and herself. She needs time with a friend or friends.

In this area each woman's capacity is different. I don't need social experiences in the same intensity a Relationships person might. I am happy with one best friend and a couple of other friends. But I still need affirmation from a close friend. I need to be able to talk honestly with a friend who knows me well enough to encourage me or correct me. I need someone to talk to about husbands and kids. And that someone is a friend.

From *Parents Magazine*, "we know that having friends is important, maybe even crucial, for good mental health," says Janet Hyde, Ph.D., professor of psychology at the University of Wisconsin-Madison. "The phone rings. It's a buddy who is also feeling down, whose toddler is whining for more juice. By the time you hang up, your equilibrium is restored."[2] As a woman, I am grateful to each of my friends. Indeed, we do get by and succeed with a little help, and sometimes a lot of help, from our friends.

Considerations

How can you choose among the good priorities that compete for your limited time? Here are some points to consider:

Go with Your Greens!

If you are offered a new opportunity that is solidly in your Green Focus area but which you are too busy to accept, consider giving up something you are already doing before saying no. One reason for this is that you may be able to replace a Red with a Green, and that is almost always good. Saying no to Reds will definitely simplify your life. If this is a long-term commitment of time and energy, it would be especially wise to say no (firmly, yet politely). You need to evaluate your time and activities in the light of your Greens. If you concentrate on your Greens you will be self-motivated, you will be encouraging to those you work for or with, you will be content, you will do a good job, and you will stick with it.

Work Environment

The Green Light Concept means more than just using your Greens. As in any job, the job of motherhood can be affected by other factors. Your work can be frustrated by many factors. These factors may or may not cause you to say no to an opportunity. The opportunity may so fit your Green that you will say yes regardless of the negatives.

For example, you may say no to an opportunity because you don't mesh well with the person in charge of the group or organization. If you don't have the same philosophy or goals, then it may be tough working with that person or organization. This principle also applies to someone you will be working closely with. You may not be able to pinpoint exactly why you don't get along with a particular person, but that is OK; interpersonal chemistry is not always tangible, identifiable, explainable, or even logical, but it's real.

Perhaps you have a supervisor who doesn't appreciate your work efforts, doesn't know your skills and strengths, or doesn't realize your potential. If any of these are the case, then your supervisor assigns you jobs that you don't enjoy doing and don't do well. That can be a source of frustration and make you want to quit. If that happens frequently, then you are most likely in the wrong job.

Another reason for wanting to say no could be your frustration with the work environment. Perhaps the organization is usually short of money and consequently does not have funds to purchase the necessary equipment to make the job enjoyable and hassle-free. Maybe there are always too few workers to do the work. In other words, the workplace itself may grate with your Reds.

Most organizations set goals for their employees. Do you feel comfortable with the goals set for you? Do those goals enable you to use your Greens? Even still, most people like some input into their work and in deciding expectations. If you are unable to communicate your goals and expectations, you may feel frustration as a result.

Me

Do you feel qualified to do the job? Even though it may be in line with your Green Light Profile, you may lack confidence to say yes to an opportunity. You may be very qualified for a certain job yet not know it because your self image is so poor. It may take some time to gain confidence in your abilities. You may need friendly encouragement from a good friend. And you may need some additional training.

Recently I was asked to take on more responsibility in the mothers' group where I volunteer. At first I thought that I should take on the new responsibility since the mothers' support group is important to me. And the person who holds this position carries a little extra prestige, which was initially appealing to me. But the more I thought about it, the more I got a knot in my stomach that wouldn't go away. Was I suffering from low self-esteem, or was I not in sync with the job? After reviewing my GLC Profile, I realized that the opportunity was not me. The position was for a Relationships and Tasks woman. At other times my lack of self confidence has been my downfall. When I could have said yes to an opportunity, I've said no, later regretting my decision. But in this case I needed to say no.

Self-esteem is not what I *really* am, but how I perceive myself to be. If I am qualified to handle the responsibilities for a position but do not take it, it's an indication of poor self-esteem.

To determine if low self-esteem is holding you back from an opportunity that fits you, ask some questions:

- ♦ Is it a match with my Green?
- ♦ Do I have training or on the job experience for this position?
- ♦ Do I really want this position and have the time to pursue it?
- ♦ Can I do this job without compromise of my values?

If the answers to those questions are all yes and you don't accept the position, you may be suffering from low self-esteem.

If you have reservations about your expertise and what is needed for the position, see if your boss would agree to one-on-one training for a while or additional courses to bring you up to speed. Remember that there is always a learning curve in any job; it takes time to fit into the organization and to figure out your place. The time of adjustment may be uncomfortable, but many employers realize this and adapt their expectations accordingly.

The final question involves your values, convictions, and morals. If your convictions need to be put aside for a job or a volunteer activity, then you will not feel comfortable doing it. An opportunity that clashes with your values is a no for you even if it fits with your GLC Profile.

Reasons I May Feel Compelled to Do Too Much

It Won't Get Done Unless

If I don't do it, it won't get done. Ever feel that way? Sometimes I do. Maybe some jobs should not be done. Sometimes (actually most days!) my beds don't get made or the dusting doesn't get done. Honestly, those are not tops on my priority list. At other times my husband makes what I think are unreasonable requests of my time. I tell him no (in a roundabout way) by saying, "Why don't you do it?" He usually sees my point. If it's that important to him, he will find the time to do it himself. But if it's not worth his time, then it's not worth his wife's time either. I'd rather be writing. I don't want to crowd my schedule with activities done out of obligation or guilt (or both).

My Child Is Involved—I Must Help Out

Here's a potential area of guilt for many moms. Most kids are involved in so many activities that for *each* of them you can be asked to do too much. You may be asked to bake cookies, give rides, be a room mother—anything, you name it. And since your kids are involved, you feel you really should help. "How can I refuse? After all, my children are involved in this activity." Yet there are times you have to say no. Saying no doesn't make you a bad mother; it's just that your time and energy are finite. And a lot of your "extra" time and energy is already devoted to good commitments.

The Kids Need These Activities

In this country we can give our children many advantages, such as activities, sports, and extra classes. These options are wonderful for your kids, providing that you do not overdo it and over schedule. To a point they provide exposure to the child's Green and to opportunities for socialization. But where do you draw the line for your family? There are days I live more in my minivan than in my home. I pack the van, drive, unpack, and do it all over again, all day long.

One way to avoid being asked to help with your child's activities is to not have so many. Few kids' activities take place in their immediate neighborhood. Sometimes you need to say enough is enough. As a mom, you need to limit the activities for the sake of your children and the entire family. Evaluate your kids' activities using your family equation. For each extra activity ask yourself, "How is the family doing because of this activity?" Many families have gotten off the merry-go-round by limiting extra activities.

Her Birthday Comes Only Once a Year

Even though she was only four years old, I spent oodles of time on my daughter's last three birthday parties. Last year I went all out on "The Little Mermaid." Finding a store that had the hats, cups, plates, and napkins was just the beginning. I used my cake decorating skills to make a double-sized cake, complete with all of the major characters from the movie. No party is complete without a game, so I made my own "Pin the Tail on the Mermaid." Little did I know how much work it would be to cut out twelve mermaid tails from mermaid-green construction paper. And no party is complete without a craft. This activity was even more time-consuming, as I cut out the figures from a roll of "Little Mermaid" wrapping paper and ran from store to store buying confetti to stand in as seaweed, stickers for sea creatures, tiny sea shells, and other choice tidbits. This party occurred one scant week before Christmas.

Ever overdo it like that? As a mom I bet you have. I don't regret having done that party. I used my creativity and the kids had a blast. However, this year I'm looking into renting out a room at a local children's museum and buying an ice-cream cake. I'll go all out on the favors, but lower my standards for the other aspects of the party. I'll appreciate paying out money to give myself a break during the holiday season.

It's the Holiday Season

Many people are saying no to holiday activities because of the frenzied pace and the pressure to spend money. It's very avant-garde to make holidays simpler. But not everyone wants to do less of everything. As with the rest of your life, what exactly will you say yes and no to during the holiday season? Let your yeses and noes reflect the values that you have and your GLC Profile, and tell the world that you love the people in your family and your friends.

It's fashionable in this anti-materialism decade to buy less expensive Christmas and Chanukah presents. Some families even desire to make all of their own presents. But GLC caution here: only those who love to do it should try. Do you know how much stress it is to make something to be ready for Christmas and good enough to give as a gift if making things is a Red? The thought is a nice one for some presents, for some people. Some Ideas people shine in this area; others dabble.

We've all thought it would be wonderful to bake Christmas goodies each year. One mom I know didn't because she is too busy with two little boys and part-time work. She said no politely and firmly when she was asked to make cookies, as they would have taken too much time for her to prepare. Instead she chose to buy quality bakery items. Money is indeed buying time for her other priorities. Trish simplifies her baking by baking cookie bars. This past year I altered her suggestion by buying inexpensive packaged cookies and putting simple decorations on each cookie. I saved oodles of time versus rolling and cutting and baking dozens of cookies.

Even though I am an Ideas woman, I didn't have time last year for all of my traditional preparations. It was a minor source of irritation not to do those activities for the holidays. But sometimes all of us need some quick and easy shortcut recipes. I have a number of them that are as easy as putting all the ingredients together, mixing and baking. No one knows that I didn't kill myself just to make a dessert that is going to be devoured in fifteen minutes.

I hear complaints about too many parties to attend. Relationships people love parties. Let them get in as many as they can. Why should they cut back? They'll love to make more time for parties as they are wonderful opportunities to get together with friends and to make new friends. Parties are definitely a Green for Relationships folks. The rest of us will have to pick and choose carefully and wisely.

The holidays are a special time for creating memories and teaching children the true meaning of the time being set aside. Ideas people will like to teach their children about the season. This past Christmas I made a cloth nativity set from a fabric panel. I did an activity in my Yellow area, sewing, so that I could do a Green, teaching my kids about the birth of Jesus.

In conclusion, your Green Light Profile plays a role in how you celebrate holidays. You should try to squeeze in some of your Greens wherever you can. People play a big role in holidays; you have to be more careful not to offend others while seeking to meet your own needs. You may also need to look for ways to save time, money, or both.

Develop an Evaluation System

For all opportunities that come my way, I think through or write down the answers to the following questions:

- ♦ Is this job responsibility or volunteer activity a green for me?
- ♦ What exactly is involved, what will I be doing? List three major job duties.
- ♦ How much time per week will this take?
- ♦ What if it takes longer than this amount of time? Who will finish the work?
- ♦ How long am I committing myself for?

Then I say, "I need a while to think about this opportunity," specifying the amount of time I need. I usually say a day for a short time commitment and at least a few days for a longer-term commitment. If the person asking needs an answer right away, especially for a long-term commitment, I'll often say, "I'm not available and I do not wish to do this."

Otherwise, after thinking about the proposed opportunity, I call the person, telling him or her my decision, and stick to it. If I decide to decline the opportunity, I practice saying the word *no* firmly. I do no one a favor, particularly myself, by saying yes when I've determined through careful thought that I should say no.

If you say yes to an opportunity, be very clear about your responsibilities and time commitment. Put it in writing as a reminder to yourself and to the person seeking help. If you still think a job will take longer than specified, add a qualifier: "I'll try this job for six months and keep track of how many hours it takes me. If it's much longer than the number of hours I can give, I'll not be able to continue doing this job."

The way you say no can reflect your future interest in helping and your time restraints. If you feel you won't ever want to work for this organization, your response could be, "Thank you for asking, but it's not something I'm interested in." However, if you are interested but are flat out overloaded with current responsibilities, you could say, "Thank you for your interest and your kind offer, but right now I'm committed to work for such and such." You could even add the phrase, "I would like to be considered in a year or two." Perhaps you don't want an ongoing commitment but would like to help the organization periodically; then your answer could be, "I can't serve weekly (or monthly), but please do feel free to call me for one-day projects or special events."

I tend to say yes to short-term or fill-in positions not in my Greens in the following cases:

- ◆The person asking has faithfully served in this area and needs some additional fill-in help.
- ◆I like the person, or the person is a friend.
- ◆It's something I have a tender spot in my heart for but would not devote lots of time to (such as baking Christmas cookies for homeless kids, building part of a house with Habitat for Humanity, or providing part of a meal for the local soup kitchen).

Relationships women almost always have a hard time saying no, especially if the person asking is someone they admire or know well. These women feel as though they will offend the asker by saying no. Relationships people have the tendency to base decisions more on feelings than on their Green and Yellow Focus areas.

Tasks people are not as affected by what people think. Instead, they often take a long time deciding what to do. They are more likely to base a decision on understanding their Greens, Yellows, and Reds.

Strategy people are likely to respond quickly to a request. They know what their goal is and will say no to what does not fit into their plans. They will tend to say no unabashedly and unashamedly. Worrying about what others think of them is rarely a problem.

Ideas people are likely to think about an opportunity for a while before giving a decision. They will think about where it could lead. They will wonder about ideas to contribute and if there will be enough creativity in the opportunity. They will have a hard time deciding and should rely heavily on their Green Light Profile for guidance.

Composing a Life

Think of the people you know and admire for their work. Have you thought of three or four people? I admire people who do fewer rather than more activities. Specifically, these people focus their energies and do one or two jobs well. They have made a decision to concentrate their efforts.

An extreme example of focused lifestyle is Mother Teresa. Her legacy will be helping the poor people of Calcutta—nothing glamorous, but focused. In Jean Fleming's book, *Between Walden and the Whirlwind* (a book I highly recommend to mothers), the author cautions us, "The question is not, How can I do more? but, Am I doing the right thing?"[3]

As an Ideas person I have trouble focusing on just one or two priorities. Like a child who enters a candy store and wants every treat she sees, I'm attracted to many of the opportunities that vie for my attention. Strategy and Tasks people tend to be more focused on one or two life goals.

In the coming years, I predict we will see more of an emphasis on concentrating our efforts. I heard a speaker, Jerry White, say that we don't need "more people to do more things, but...more people doing fewer of the right things."[4] Doing fewer of the right things leaves you time for your Greens and for your lifetime dreams. As you learn to say no, especially to your Reds, you will have more time. This time could be used to pursue your lifetime dream, or something else you've wanted to do for a long time. I like the words of Gandhi: "There is more to life than increasing its speed."

At the end of my life I want the time I've devoted to activities to speak loudly and clearly about my values, priorities, and commitments. Time is too precious to fritter away or have someone else decide how to spend it for me. A Bible verse that best conveys my thoughts is Ephesians 5:15: "Live life, then, with a due sense of responsibility, not as people who do not know the meaning and purpose of life but as those who do" (PH). My life may not be spectacular, but it is one that I have chosen where I had a choice, and it does show my commitments and my loves.

Borrow a Two-year-old

Need a refresher course on how to say no? If you don't have a two-year-old of your own, find one that you can borrow. It shouldn't be too hard—most moms of two-year-olds will willingly part with them for a while. Particularly note their insistence when saying the word no. Memorize that behavior. Oh yes, when you imitate the intensity of their no, remember to add the tact you've learned in adulthood. Most of all, I hope you enjoy seeing the benefits of saying no because it will leave you the time to pursue the lifetime dreams in your life. Unless you learn to say no, you may never know those benefits.

PART SEVEN

Maintaining Realistic Expectations Through Balance

Chapter 12

Moms Have Other Needs Too

◆

We flipped mindlessly through the TV channels after wrestling the kids to bed. Exhausted after a long day, my husband and I hoped to watch a mindless sitcom. Instead, we experienced a visual delight as we witnessed the last twenty minutes of a juggler's one hour show. I've seen ordinary kind of juggling—the ball, bowling pin, and bean bag variety. But I've never seen this type before. Juggling had risen to an art form when performed by this man. He juggled everything imaginable while walking, climbing steps, and sitting. Mesmerized by the ease and flow with which he performed, I was awed by his grand finale, for which he juggled softball-sized glass balls, telling a story of birth, living, and surrender through his movements.

Juggling my life is nothing like his performance. I do it neither beautifully nor with ease. Certainly no one would mistake it for art. But as a woman, the people and areas I juggle are far more fragile and precious than glass balls. You've already considered many areas that you juggle. In this chapter I'll cover two more important areas, namely the body and the spirit. Others have done a more thorough and detailed job of writing about them, but they are too important to bypass here. Besides, we'll apply the Green Light Concept to them too.

The Body

Before I had children, I couldn't understand why moms seemed to put on weight and have a tendency to look out of shape after having a couple of kids. I thought, *How could they let themselves get so frumpy looking?* I thought I'd never look like that, having been a beanpole most of my life, tall and thin. I did a lot of sports as a child—softball and tennis were my favorites. This trend continued into college as I exercised nearly every day, playing varsity tennis and softball. Despite my busy schedule in engineering school, I was able to make exercising a priority.

But now I not only have kids, I also have a large house that requires a lot of time, a husband I short-change out of time too frequently, part-time paid work, and volunteer work for my mother's group. Exercise has not been a consistent priority since children entered the equation.

After having gotten very out of shape after two pregnancies, I attempted to make my body look healthier and trimmer and make my body more aerobically healthy. For about six months, I walked briskly for about forty-five minutes a day, three times a week. Sometimes I made time enough to do the Nautilus machines, but mostly I ran in for a quick workout between mothering responsibilities. I felt wonderful and my postpregnancy tummy and legs were getting firmed up. I felt as if I had more energy. The exercise experts have the supporting facts to show that, indeed, I did have more energy.

That was before my youngest child was constantly sick this winter. Every week he has something else: a cold, an ear infection, flu, bronchitis. Having a sick child awake at night kept me awake at night too. And so, I reverted to napping in the afternoons. My exercise time went out the window. I knew I ought to exercise. I knew I should do it because I am overweight. But since then I have not readjusted my schedule to make it fit.

So how can I encourage you that exercise is beneficial to your health, when I myself am not doing it? I can merely say that I understand why moms cannot seem to fit exercise into their schedules; it isn't urgent or necessary. Exercise is important, though. All of us know it is. While I'm tempted to use the dreaded word *should*, I won't. Yet, in the coming months I hope that both of us can somehow fit some exercise into our busy lives and busy schedules.

It may be discouraging even to try. You know you will miss some times because of kids being sick, too many responsibilities, and mini-emergencies that crop up. And when you do start exercising, you'll be tempted to compare yourself with others in the length of time and quality of workout. Unlike childless people, you won't be able to do a complete workout all (or most) of the time.

Yet some exercise is better than no exercise. Also, you need to know that it takes time to get back into shape. I took six years to get out of shape, so it will take more than a couple of months before I notice a return to my former self.

Do people with different Green Light Profiles view exercise differently? You bet. As an Ideas person, it was fun learning about exercise, how to do it and how it benefits me. My Yellow is Tasks, so I concentrate on that area when I exercise—doing it better, more precisely, keeping my head straight and my posture correct, noticing improvements in my body (fewer inches around the thighs and hips). When I'm on the treadmill, I enjoy talking and walking with another person. I can learn about the person, or learn something from him or her.

Relationships people are more apt to continue with exercising if they find a faithful friend to exercise with, perhaps joining a health club where there are plenty of people. Since they are naturally companion/coach type people, they are the ones who encourage you while you are exercising. And they love it when you encourage them when they are exercising. They don't like intense competition.

A Strategy person will exercise as long as she can see results. She will set goals in her exercising, wanting to be the fastest, the fittest, and the best. As such she will gravitate toward the competitive sports and the league ladders of racquetball, tennis, squash, and handball. A Strategy person tends to be the coach-to-win type coach; she is the motivator on the team. Some Strategy people are uniquely designed for mountain climbing, marathons, and triathlons—so different from the aerobic classes, where Relationships types love to get to know people. Is either one better? No, just very different.

A Tasks person likes exercise that can be constantly improved upon and made better. For example, she enjoys routine exercise programs; as she repeats her routine over and over, she does them more precisely and more correctly. Tennis is good for Tasks people, and so are the Nautilus machines. A Tasks person loves the standard, repetitious exercises and the charts she can fill out as the exercises are completed. Additionally, she likes to exercise alone. She doesn't need encouragement from other people. She sets her own goals and measures her own progress.

An Ideas person initially enjoys the whole aspect of exercising and keeping fit because she is learning so much. But her motivation does not last long, and she may need to vary exercise routines and activities, or exercise at different locations with different people, to keep the newness going. She'll spend exercise time thinking of ideas or contemplating a design. Her attention may turn to what people are wearing so she can contemplate other designs. Perhaps she'll stimulate her mind by listening to tapes or reading while on an exercise machine so that she can "learn while she burns." But she will get bored with the day in and day out repetition. Exercising just isn't cerebral enough.

Rest and Sleep

Looking at this area through Green Light lenses is not black and white. Many factors out of your control influence why you do or don't get enough rest. As a mom, you know that children disrupt your sleep patterns for quite some time after they are born. They awaken because of hunger, a bowel movement, a bad dream, teething, illness, or a sudden urge to play with Mom. Children require differing amounts of sleep based on their own internal clocks. Naps may be long, short, or nonexistent, even soon after birth. What I can suggest is try to get the amount of sleep that you—your body and mind—need as consistently as you possibly can. You will be healthier and better able to deal with kids, love your husband, and do volunteer activities, work, and other activities.

Executives like to pat themselves on the back for working harder and achieving more than other people. Many people believe they are more motivated and work harder and perhaps sleep less than the rest of us. Let us now dispel that myth. We are all motivated to do or be a certain way. People whose Green is Relationships work hard in their relationships with people. They would readily stay up late to talk, to counsel or to care for others. For an Ideas person, a new book or an unfinished quilt are temptation enough to stay up into the early hours. Tasks people tends to get carried away with the details of projects that they are working on, and the hours can quickly pass by without them knowing it. A person operating in his or her Green Focus area needs no motivation to perform.

Green activities rejuvenate you; you could do them all day and all night, though that would not be good for your body. Whatever your schedule and the schedules of your children, getting the amount of sleep that you need is vital. Tasks people are at an advantage in this regard because they are apt to go by the book. They tend to complete tasks correctly and to be more conscientious about getting enough sleep. A Strategy person, on the other hand, is more apt to do far too many activities.

"Parents must learn to monitor their own physical tolerance, replenishing and conserving their strength for the long haul,"[1] cautions James Dobson, Ph.D. Since parenting is for the long haul, you need your sleep. As quoted from *Reader's Digest*, "If it is sleep that knits up the raveled sleeve of care, then an overwhelming number of Americans are walking around with distinctly tatty shirt cuffs."[2] Adequate sleep is one way to provide care for you, the caregiver. It is a necessity.

Indulgences

Every person has an area of weakness. One woman's "Ben and Jerry's" is another's "Pepperidge Farm Distinctive Cookies." A need for moderation is seen in many of the health reports and diet magazines. There is a discrepancy between what is and what should be. We know what we should do; it's not a question of knowledge, but of practice and habit and saying no.

As women we know that our indulgences and excesses are due in large part to our emotions. Anorexia, bulimia, compulsive overeating, overeating, and bingeing result from emotional attachment to food rather than from hunger pangs. It's not easy, but all of us must take care of what goes into our bodies. This may have to start with facing the truth about what makes us overindulge.

Our emotions affect how and why we do these things to ourselves. Some of the most helpful insights I've read about substance abuse and food abuse have to do with the meaning that we attach to food or whatever we overdo. Many of the self-help programs focus on the motivation for overeating or for doing drugs. Without getting at the root cause of the problem, other methods do not work well. The root of the problem may be from childhood experiences, PMS, or other causes. Many times it's related to functioning in Red areas for too long. Oprah Winfrey was right when she said, "Dieting is not about weight. It's about everything else that's not going right in your life."[3]

Clothes and Finishing Touches

What is comfortable and appropriate for you based on your lifestyle? Do you need to dress up to be appropriate? Then do so. Do you want to dress up because that is the kind of person you are? Then do so. Are you comfortable in pants and sweaters? Then dress that way. I know my favorite clothes are a pair of shorts with a shirt and my casual, flat, walking shoes with a pair of white socks. When the weather gets cooler I put on an oversized sweater. People who know me know it's cold when I have on a pair of pants. But if I have a party or function to attend where the hostess will be dressed, then I alter my dress significantly to accommodate the dress level of my hostess. After all, she is taking the time and effort to throw a wonderful party, to set the mood, and to make all of the preparations. Dressing up is the least I can do. As you adapt to the people around you, do not change your style of dress; only change the levels of casualness or dressiness. You need to be yourself.

A Relationships person appreciates it when you notice what she is wearing and compliment her positively on it. She will be apt to compliment you on how you look in a new dress. She will go to the make-up booth for a makeover, to fashion shows, or to shopping centers with a friend.

A Tasks woman may like to experiment with clothes to try to improve the look. She may also like to organize her closet and make-up so she can get ready quickly with little notice. She likes her clothes to fit properly and correctly and she is apt to have her clothes tailored. She might buy inexpensive clothes and accessories or those in need of repair to improve them. As she builds her wardrobe, she tends to save money by sticking to basic colors and classic styles. She tends to dress conservatively rather than innovatively. Therefore, she doesn't need to change clothes with each new style, saving her money and time.

The trend setters in fashion are some Ideas women and some Relationships women; both of them tend to make customized designs so that they are not wearing what everyone else is wearing.

A Strategy woman can overdo her efforts on fashion and make-up. She would probably be apt to get "the works"—hair, perm, and nails—done at one place (to get quick results). She can do the same thing with clothes, preferring to buy an outfit new with all the accessories at the same time. Coordinated from head to toe, she feels that she is selling herself when people see her and she wants the best. She appreciates looking at others who are the same way. She does not like fixing or mending things. If she finds a man she wants to impress, look out—she'll do it using all these methods. A Strategy woman goes for the executive look, the look that gives an aura of command and authority. She often chooses power colors.

An Ideas woman, if she works with fabrics, may design her own clothes or use a pattern and make her own clothes. She is creative. Other women admire her work and wish they could do what she does, but it's not their Green. She adds just the right touches of details and picks out just the right colors and fabrics.

If not involved in sewing and fabrics, an Ideas woman is too busy reading and learning to be concerned about her dress and appearance much. At some time in her life, she may make a point to learn about fashion and apply what she learns. She may prefer casual or earthy dress, or perhaps the intellectual and collegiate look. She dresses more for comfort and function than just for looks.

The Spirit

Quiet

A mom needs quiet time because her house is so noisy with children, and her life is so busy and complicated. Anytime I get the chance, I love to listen to nothing. I don't use the radio much when driving in the car; I savor the sound of silence. Since becoming a mom, I like the Simon and Garfunkel song by the same name. For the tough days I might even say, like Shakespeare,

"Silence is the perfect herald of joy."[4] At the end of the day my ears hurt from hearing too much fighting, whining, and endless chatter. When the lights are out and I can lie in bed and hear nothing, I feel refreshed. For moms, the sound of silence, from time to time, is to be savored and enjoyed.

Something More

There is more to life than the fulfillment that comes from using your Greens. There is a deeper quiet than mere physical silence; a more complete acceptance than your husband or best friends can provide. You and I need an inner peace to help us through the many times of turmoil. We need to feel unconditional acceptance and love. An overall very good life is still missing something. Perhaps Hugo de Anima said it best when he said, "The heart is a small thing, but desireth great matters . . . the whole world is not sufficient for it."[5]

So far I've spent so much time on the mind, on being fulfilled and using your Green and Yellow Focus areas as much as possible, that I am afraid I have overdone it. Every book must have an emphasis, as does this one. But using the Green Light Concept will not necessarily fulfill you. You can use nothing but Greens and still feel empty inside. You may have the fulfillment that having a wonderful husband, good kids, a nice home, and material possessions bring—yet not have peace and rest.

While I believe fulfillment and the Green Light Concept are important, they're not all-important. There is something more.

Having your little ones grow up can cause you to wonder more about the something that is missing in your life. What are you to do when your kids are asking you questions you want to answer with confidence but can only guess at? Perhaps you'd like spiritual values to fit into your life, but they don't seem to now. You're not sure what you believe.

We're talking about the spiritual aspect of life. "None but God can satisfy the longing of an immortal soul; that as the heart was made for Him, so He only can fill it."[6] Many people know what that longing feels like. Yet some don't know how to satisfy it. And some who know forget often and need reminding. I am in the latter group.

Improved Lives

Whatever group you find yourself in, you may feel that your family life would be easier and better if daycare were adequate, affordable (or subsidized), and of a higher quality (higher adult-to-child ratio). However, one poll I think better describes what families, especially moms, are looking for, and it's not better daycare. *Family Circle* published the results. Women were asked how their lives could be improved. Of the people who responded, 56 percent said their families would be better with "religious values." Daycare issues were at the bottom of the list for making the family better, at a mere 2 percent.[7] It's not just what you have in life that counts, it's what you don't have in a relationship with God that is important.

You may hesitate to turn to God because you feel that you can handle your own affairs pretty well. Or you've seen some people who use religion as a crutch. Certainly some people do. They put their brains in neutral and expect God to do what they themselves could do. But God doesn't want that. Just as you don't want to do for your children what they are capable of doing on their own, God wants you to do what you are able to do for yourself.

Or you may be afraid that getting close to God will somehow alter your personality, that all people close to

God have a "religious" personality. All through this book I've respected the variety of styles and personalities that people have, as well as the differing decisions and applications that people make. God loves them all and He has no favorites. God designed all personalities. If we begin to have a relationship with Him, He'll not take away the unique design He gave us.

It's OK to have doubts and questions when seeking God. They are part of the process. Don't let anyone force you into a decision before you are satisfied with the answers to your questions. But you need to concentrate on more than only knowing yourself and how you're designed. The spiritual life is about knowing God. For He is your designer, your creator.

Gap

Some people feel that they have to get their lives a little bit more together before they can have a relationship with God. I'm talking about the gaps between what people would like to be and do, and how they really are. A mother knows about the gap between Perfect Mother and what she really is. Everyone has some area or areas that they feel are less than perfect.

Like me, your area of weakness may be that you yell at your kids or that you hold a grudge against your husband when he neglects to talk to you or take you out on a date night. God calls all such actions and attitudes sins, a seldom-used word in our culture. If you'd like, you can refer to them as doing wrong or not being perfect. The Bible says that sins "have made a separation between you and your God" (Isaiah 59:2, NASB).

Being the person I am, I don't like to think that I sin. My first response to my wrongdoing is denial—to excuse it in a number of different ways. Sometimes I blame it on PMS. Other times I say I'm having a bad day, or I blame my actions on my husband's actions. Or I tell myself I'd do better if my kids were more manageable. But deep down inside I know that it is I who am wrong. Will I admit it to myself? And if I do, what can I do about it?

There is only one person who can help me to do something about my weaknesses. The person of Jesus Christ lived on the earth for 33 short years, a life long enough to have done wrong but which included none. He wasn't a recluse from the world, hiding out in a sanctuary either. I think He experienced what you and I as moms experience—He met a lot of people's needs, taking care of the sick, and putting in a lot of hours. At times He was exhausted; at times He was happy; at times He mourned; and at times He was hungry. Yes, He was real and around other people a lot. But He didn't sin.

So was He here to show us that it is possible to be perfect if only we try hard enough? No. He came so that God could identify with us. In the biblical account of Jesus' birth, an angel spoke in a dream to Joseph: "'Call His name Immanuel,' which translated means, 'God with us'" (Matthew 1:23, NASB). God came to live among us for a while so that we would know that He knows what we experience in life. While He was here, He laughed, cried, wept, got angry, was disappointed in people, and loved people. And the amazing truth is that He didn't sin.

Christ bridged that gap for us between what we'd like to be and what we are. Because of His death and resurrection, Christ has given me the opportunity to be like Him. My brain cannot comprehend this fact fully, and as a person who likes to know (an Ideas person) that kind of bothers me, but I believe it.

My belief is strengthened by realizing that Jesus Christ is different from all other religious founding leaders. Like other leaders, such as Gandhi, Buddha, and Mohammed, Jesus is compassionate, human, a servant, and a man of moral standards. I admire a lot of these leaders for these actions and qualities. Yet none of those others were sinless. In fact, Jesus is God. And still the biggest reason to believe in Jesus is that no other leader has been resurrected from the dead, a fact unique to Jesus. He is the only founder of a religion that has a claim to resurrection. So I too, like Peter, one of Jesus' disciples, have said, "Who else should we go to? Your words have the ring of eternal life!" (John 6:68, PHILLIPS). Jesus offers us Himself, as well as eternal life.

A Parent's Heart

When I came to Jesus, I believed that He was the Son of God who came to earth to live among us and be our example. I believed Him to be a good teacher. And with my heart, I believed that He is the one who died on the cross so that I would no longer be separated from God. I couldn't make myself complete; it took Christ's death and resurrection to do that for me. I like Rebecca Manley Pippert's explanation of what God did:

> The parent's heart is to stand in for the child. Stand in for the child? There is our clue. When love comes face-to-face with crisis and suffering in the one who is loved, its first impulse is to stand in, to substitute. . . . But that is exactly what God felt. And that is exactly what God did. He took our place.[8]

The Bible puts it this way: "God is on one side and all the people on the other side, and Christ Jesus, himself man, is between them to bring them together" (1 Timothy 2:5, TLB).

There is a part in the Bible that describes a loving parent-and-child relationship. It's one of my favorites. It tells of a young man who asks his dad for his inheritance money. Could you imagine doing that to your parents? Amazingly, the father gives his son the money. The young man leaves home to live it up in the big city. Penniless and destitute after squandering all and working as practically a slave, he soon comes to his senses. He decides to return home and ask his dad's forgiveness.

Meanwhile, the father has been waiting for his son, looking for him. The key phrase is, "while he was still a long way off, his father saw him" (Luke 15:20, NASB). The father did not make the child return all the way home, but kept looking for his son. When the young man was in sight, the father ran to greet him. And what a greeting he got! It's an all-out party and celebration. He is given new clothes, "the best robe," and a ring that symbolized full belonging and membership in the family once again. The father forgave his wayward son (Luke 15:11-32).

Is it just a great story? Not at all. It tells of a God who looks for us a long way off and meets us. We don't have to have it all together. It tells of a God who is eager to forgive. That is what God does for us when we see the need for Him in our own lives. It tells of a God that desires that we be part of His family, along with all of the rewards and privileges, so much so that Jesus died for our sins. No abuse. No manipulation. Just acceptance and love, with none of the limitations and weaknesses of our human parents.

God is our parent. He knows that we don't have it all together. He does not expect that. He'll love you even when you yell at the kids, when you're not speaking to your husband because you're mad at him, when you shirk taking care of the house, when you feel like a failure, and even when you don't love yourself. No matter what, He'll love you. He doesn't expect you to be perfect, just to be honest with Him.

An often-quoted verse from the Bible is, "the truth shall set you free!" (John 8:32, NASB). The truth that Jesus died on the cross for you will set you free. The next time you see a cross, remember that the separation between God and you has been bridged.

Our Caretaker

What a relief that we don't have to be perfect. God loves and accepts us just as we are. In all of our frenzied, busy, and sometimes frustrating lives, we can have the peace of Jesus. His peace is "nothing like the peace of this world" (John 14:27, PH). Peace from Him doesn't fade away with a failed dream or a strong-willed child or a difficult marriage. His peace is not based on circumstances, but on knowing that we are invited into God's family because He has accepted and loved us. With His acceptance and love, He does take care of us.

Also, God left us with the Bible so that we can have some help raising our children, loving our husbands, and handling the uncertainties of life. If you'd like to find out more about how Jesus lived His short life on this earth, what He did, and how He showed He was the perfect human, compassionate God, I recommend that you read a book of the Bible called Luke. Luke was a doctor who lived during the time of Jesus, and he recorded as an eyewitness all that he saw Jesus do and say.

When reading the Bible, read it as you would any other book. Take as fact those events and statements that are presented as fact. Know that it's a story or an object lesson when you read the word "parable." Mostly, read the Bible as you would read a letter from your best friend who loves you, knows you well, and wants the best for you.

I believe that your relationship with Jesus will be shaped by what your strengths and weaknesses are, but I cannot say exactly how. God is so powerful and mighty and creative and unique, and such a good teacher and encourager, that I cannot know how God will reveal Himself to you in your life. He will use people, such as your husband, your children, your neighbors, your relatives, and your friends. He will use circumstances, perhaps even job layoffs and moves and deaths and illnesses and good times. He will use your past and how you were brought up. He will work in infinite ways and means. I hope that someday you will put your trust in Him. In the meantime, I hope that you will be attentive to God in your life.

Something More

Remember the first time you met your best friend? You couldn't know at the time that she would become your best friend, yet over time she did. All relationships take time to develop. While we spend time together communicating, we develop a relationship based on knowledge and trust. The same will be true of you if you decide to enter into a relationship with God. It will take time. I know He wants to have a relationship with you; He sent Christ to show it. He is waiting and watching for you, as the father waited for his child. Don't settle merely for "doing your Greens" when God offers so much more.

Chapter 13

Boomeranging Back to Church

---◆---

"Just when we thought we were doing something different," said my friend. Her brother-in-law had recently told her about an article in a weekly news magazine detailing the baby boomer generation's return to church in record numbers.

Our conversation had turned to the topic of churches because I was impressed with Lynn's church. For their Halloween party, they served a meal, played games, and carved pumpkins. I love to hear about a church that is pro-family not only with words but with deeds. As our children played in the indoor McDonald's playground, we had a chance to talk about what we liked about our churches, comparing them to the churches we had attended as children.

As youngsters, my husband Dave and I had grown up in church-going families, but between adolescence and young adulthood we had dropped off church attendance for a while and dropped out emotionally. Yes, we both had now boomeranged back to church. Like a boomerang—which is thrown, covers a large trajectory, and then returns to its point of origin—we had returned. According to Newsweek this has been a trend of our generation. "At one time or another, roughly two-thirds of baby boomers dropped out of organized religion. But in recent years, more than a third of the dropouts have returned."[1] Everyone is doing it.

Everyone Is Doing It

Just how many people can be called baby boomers? According to Paul C. Light, "The number of women having at least two children increased by half between the 1930s and 1950s, resulting in a demographic wedge of 75 million children. It was a sea of babies, with one wave of four million babies after another every year for a decade...a seemingly endless line of babies."[2] And there are many parents in their twenties not officially part of the baby boom generation who have returned to church after an absence.

In a way it can be a little discouraging being in such a big population group. It's possible to feel as if you are never doing something unique. In fact, it can seem as if you are doing just what everyone else is doing.

But Dave and I aren't living as we are just because we've watched others and followed their lead. Rather, we decided for ourselves based on knowledge, planning, and strategizing, taking into account our families' needs. For example, when we refinanced our home we were aware of the falling interest rates. We calculated our savings and decided that 10 percent was reason enough to refinance. Many homeowners jumped at the chance to save *x* dollars per month on our mortgage or to convert our mortgages from a dragged-out thirty years to a more foreseeable twenty or even fifteen years.

We thought ourselves extravagant when we purchased the dishwasher, the living room set, a personal computer, and finally a minivan (little did we know the countryside would become littered with minivans). As the 1990s approached, we put the brakes on and started saving. We thought that we were smart and were doing something unique. The statistics show otherwise. "The growth of real per capita consumer spending is down from around 3.5 percent a year in the mid-Eighties to 1.9 percent last year. The savings rate bottomed out at 3.2 percent of disposable personal income in 1987 and has trended slowly upward ever since, reaching 5.2 percent recently."[3] Oh well. What else can we expect when so many people in the United States are in the same season of life?

In a similar manner, Dave and I noticed the unrest in the world, the shallowness of materialism, our yearning for something beyond what we could see. And we noticed a longing for the sense of family and community that we gave up in favor of long-distance family relations. So while young and middle-aged adults turned back, as a group, to organized religion, Dave and I did so through individual decisions.

We decided that maybe there was something valid to "organized religion"—an option many of us had ignored for a time. Perhaps this should surprise us, since in the Eighties as we watched some of the leaders in the religious arena fall; with hesitation and timidity, sometimes with glee, we witnessed their demise. Yet many of us recognized that our local church was nothing like the sham of some televangelists. We made that separation in our minds and embraced the local, while we discounted the national. As quoted from *Christianity Today*, "some religious broadcasters have created the impression that evangelical programs are sweeping the land and attracting enormous audiences. . . . It has no basis in research."[4]

Children Are a Big Reason

There is little room for doubt about why young and middle-aged adults are returning to church: children. "And the Children Shall Lead Them" was the headline on the December 17, 1990, cover of *Newsweek*. The cover article reported that, statistically, baby boomers with children are "twice as likely to join a religious congregation than those with none."[5]

But what is it about children that causes prodigal sons and daughters to return to church? Is it the miracle of life that renews faith in God? Is it a child's wide-eyed curiosity soaking up the newness of life, in contrast to our cynically toughened hearts and view on life? Perhaps we've struggled with circumstances beyond our control—a parent with Alzheimer's disease, the death of a family pet, the relocation of our company and residence—and come to realize our limited power to protect children in an uncertain world. Perhaps we have our children for such a short time that we want to give them a firm foundation for making life's tough decisions. Whatever your reason, having a child often generates interest in attending church on a regular basis.

Church Shoppers

Many in our generation have made the move back to church, and many more are thinking about it. We have or want a church that embraces us, as well as embraces our children. For this reason and others, we have been called "church shoppers." It's not meant to be a flattering term. Nonetheless, my husband and I plead guilty.

We church-shopped twice in our lives, once when we were first married and once when we lived in California for five months. The first time we knew we were in the wrong church when a woman accosted me with, "It's so nice to see young people in church." I quickly sized up the situation by glancing around. Yes, just as I had expected, I was engulfed in a sea of gray-haired parishioners. We stood out in that crowd. The tip-off should have been the parking lot, which was loaded with late-model Cadillacs, Buicks, and oversized vehicles (the median age of a Cadillac driver is 58; it used to be in the sixties[6]). While we valued and wanted a variety of age groups in a church, this one wasn't for us—they offered little for newly-marrieds and young parents—not even nursery care.

Another saying that gave us a bad feeling immediately was the little sentence, "We used to have that at our church." Churches on the verge of death were apt to use this unwelcome eulogy. To them we looked like a breath of fresh air. And they encouraged us to attend their church and bring some of those abandoned programs back to their church. However, as newlyweds planning to start a family, we decided that it wasn't our season to rebuild those troubled churches from the ground up. Rather, we were looking for a church that could meet our needs and not drain us of precious time and energy. Thus, our priority was to meet some of our needs, not to serve.

Our Needs

Family Events and Activities

We want activities offered for the whole family on a

regular basis, such as my friend's church that held a family Halloween party. Our church offers such events; we've had a family advent wreath-making night, concert picnics, and our annual summer barbecue. At all of these events children are welcome. My children can attend our Sunday school class on any Sunday and be treated with respect. In our church, children are not merely tolerated or ignored; they are welcomed and enjoyed. Indeed our church lives out the words of Jesus, "Permit the children to come to Me, and do not hinder them, for the kingdom of God belongs to such as these" (Luke 18:16, NASB).

Churches that offer family events send a message more important than having fun. They show by their deeds that they value marriages and families and want to give them a means to be strong. Sensitive churches are also discerning enough to know that not all families consist of a mom, dad, and children. Single-parent families and childless couples need acceptance and help to be strong.

Children a Priority

We don't want our children present at all times when we attend church. With preschoolers we need them in some sort of child care so that we can worship and learn. This area always causes concern for the safety, teaching, and care of our children.

Safety

Our home church in California was huge. When we entered the parking lot the first Sunday, we thought the traffic controller was weird. He held up his hand, alternating between one or two fingers pointed up. Obviously he was trying to communicate something to us. We rolled down our window to hear the verbal explanation. He said, "One service or two?" This church was so crowded that cars were parked according to your length of stay.

We parked in the appropriate section and made our way to the maze of nursery rooms. The children were put in a room based on every six months of birthdays. Hannah would be put into the July 1—Dec 31, 1986 room. We brought her to the room and tried to enter— nothing doing, no one was allowed into the room. And we were given a number tag for her and for us; without it we could not claim our child. It seemed cold to us. But it was necessary and it made us feel secure because we really didn't know anybody at that church. In the coming weeks and months we sensed care for our children by the workers, even with the tight security measures.

Teaching

We have a church that teaches our children about God in ways that they can enjoy and understand. For our children that means music, stories, and crafts. Just as we would choose a preschool, we make sure the children's activities, supplies, equipment, and toys are age appropriate. Most of the time our children play and have fun because they are young, but what they are learning, both in the content and through the teachers, is vital because their early impressions of church will stick for many years to come.

Care

"We have to leave in five minutes so we're not late," my husband reminded me. I knew that, but not only hadn't I prepared the night before, but I am half comatose until 10 A.M. We managed to rush the children through the remainder of their breakfast. I grabbed a piece of toast and a glass of water for me and dragged the kids into the minivan.

I applied my makeup on the way to church. We screeched into the parking lot and my husband dropped the kids and me off at the door; we were so late that there was parking only in the outermost parts of the lot. As we burst into the nursery, Peg greeted me and my child with, "Welcome Nathanael, it's so good to see you!" She scooped him up in her arms and calmed him down. Her smile was so contagious and so foreign to Nathan (he certainly didn't see one on my face that morning) that it captivated him. As she gently ushered me out the door she said, "Mom, you need to go to church. He'll do just fine." My sense of balance was restored. I was freed up to do what I came to do, worship God with other people.

I hope God has special blessings in mind for saints like her when they get to heaven.

Should I Bother Going to Church?

There are mornings when I would like to stay in bed and read the paper or have breakfast out with the family. Other mornings I just don't want to put up with the aggravations of the Sunday morning shuffle. But Peg, my son's child care worker, was right. I need church. It's not screaming for urgency, but it's important. It's one of the most important activities my husband and I do during the week. For while I have personal, private beliefs based on the Bible, I need other people's encouragement, help, and teaching to live out those beliefs.

Learning about God

While I, my husband, and our children benefit from the perks and benefits of attending a pro-family church, the family emphasis alone isn't enough for us. In fact, our top priority when looking for a church was to find one that respected the teachings of Jesus because we wanted to know more about Him. While we wanted answers to give to our children, we first wanted answers for ourselves. We wanted reassurances about life, everyday living, and the inevitable crises. For us that meant finding a church that accepted the Bible as truth.

In the previous chapter I wrote that I had developed a relationship with Jesus. I view church as one way to enhance my relationship with Him. A relationship is based on respect, trust, and love—which is how I'd describe my relationship with God. But it took time to get to know Him better, through church and other private times. I shy away from religion, which can tend to be a list of oughts based on obligation or fear or both.

So we were not looking for a church that wanted us to follow orders blindly from a high church authority. Rather, we wanted freedom to search and dig out answers from the Bible for ourselves.

A little of that comes from our "question authority" college days, and some comes from our Green Light Profiles—both my husband and I are Ideas people. As such we enjoy Bible study and adult Sunday school. Other characteristics that Ideas people like in a church are:

♦ Deep, thought-provoking sermons

♦ Well-decorated and aesthetically pleasing worship places (perhaps stained-glass windows or hilltop sunrise Easter services or other outdoor services)

♦ Music that coincides with the message of the day

♦ Other people who like to discuss issues, brainstorm, and have deep conversations

For Ideas people, environment and atmosphere have a big impact on their worship experience, either enhancing or detracting from it.

If you are a Relationships person, you may be wanting something entirely different. Relationships people aren't as interested in deep Bible study. Rather, they seek a warm and accepting church, which gives:

- ♦ A sense of belonging that is developed in close friendships

- ♦ An emotional worship service, in which people feel free to cry and express their emotions to God without shame, and preaching that emphasizes God's personal nature and interest in people on a personal level

- ♦ Support groups that meet weekly to help in each person's season or circumstance of life

- ♦ Sense of family, community, and closeness with other church members

Relationships people want to connect heart to heart with a group of people on a weekly, if not a daily, basis.

Tasks people, however, like to spend a minimal amount of time with other people. They tend to look for a well-organized church and worship service, perhaps more of a traditional church where there are no surprises in format or structure. They enjoy:

- ♦ Methodical, three point sermons

- ♦ Predictable services and events

- ♦ Bible studies

- ♦ Services and events that begin and end on time

Strategy people aren't interested in what other Profiles are interested in. They have little interest in setting a worshipful mood with music or special surroundings. Building relationships with others is of little importance to them. They want to see numerical results quickly and "get things done." Therefore, they don't like in-depth Bible study. They like to be instrumental in church planning. They enjoy:

- ◆Worship services that have a clear purpose
- ◆Programs and opportunities that are efficient and effectual

I cannot overemphasize the importance of values and convictions to Strategy people in this area, because church and Sunday school typically offers them little in their Green Focus area. If you are a Strategy person, you will especially want to review the other Green Light focus areas and concentrate your church involvement in your Yellow.

Lasting Value

There is no one way to structure church or to worship; your preferences are just that, preferences. Accept methods of worship and preferences that don't match your Green Light Profile. The appropriateness of the way you worship God and feel His presence does not depend on how much you learn, what you feel, how logical the sermon is to you, or how patiently you endure a service you didn't enjoy. Rather, the acid test is whether you live out in the world, especially in your home, what you have nodded in agreement to on Sunday. "In fact, the Apostle John implies that the home is the ultimate test."[7]

That means application to me. As I've spent time getting to know God, I've matured as my needs have been met. Additionally, I have a deepened care and love for people and a greater sensitivity to their needs. In short, I serve out of this sense of maturity, thankfulness, and love—not because of the dreaded "should." A verse of the Bible that echoes this thought is 1 John 3:18: "Let us not love with word or with tongue, but in deed and truth" (NASB).

Givers, Takers, and Other Kinds of Churchgoers

When Dave and I first attended church we wanted to know how that church could meet our needs. And for years it did, and the people there taught us about serving and helping others. At first we helped in little noncommittal ways, on a short-term basis or in a substitute capacity. Now we give to others on a consistent, regular basis. Because our church has met our needs and strengthened us, we are in a position to serve willingly, to contribute so that other families can be strengthened. As an example, each week I help run the mother's support program. Lately we've gone beyond just helping young couples with kids by volunteering time with international college students. And we serve out of gratitude for all God has done for us through Christ.

We choose these activities for a number of reasons. I'm involved with the mother's support group because that is the season of life I am in right now. We serve with the college students because we like being with them. Both my husband and I can learn from them—their customs and foods and cultures. We put our Greens to work as we learn about new people, groups and cultures, and spend time in the great outdoors camping and hiking. Also, we do these activities with our children. These activities fit into our family equation and with our Green Light Profiles.

Typical ways in which Ideas people help their churches are as Bible study leaders, writing the church newsletter, decorating the church, developing Bible studies, and sewing for missionaries. Ideas people like learning and experimenting with ideas and concepts, with the end product being written material, handmade items, or new knowledge.

Tasks people enjoy bookkeeping, record keeping, cleaning the building, mowing the lawn, repairing the church van, folding and stuffing the weekly bulletin, entering data on the computer, and filing. Tasks people enjoy working with things, information, data, and machines.

In contrast, Relationships people prefer to work directly with people. They are likely to enjoy doing child care, counseling, visiting shut-ins and elderly people, greeting visitors at church, hostessing parties, and making meals for new moms or ill people.

Strategy people like to use their skills and interests in influencing church policy and future direction. As such, these women are usually effective promoting a program and getting people excited about it. They like to be instrumental in helping the church develop long-range plans. For example, they are likely to undertake a stewardship program or to spearhead a church building program. Also, speaking to groups is solidly in their Green.

Each Green Light Profile has a place in God's service.

Perfect Church

Bet you can tell that I don't have a problem with the consumerism of shopping for a church. It would be unwise not to do so with so many churches available in many communities close to home (which is another matter for you and your husband to settle upon). While I advocate checking out churches to find the one that suits your family's needs, I don't recommend continual church switching. Settle into one, put down roots, and enjoy the family called your church.

Realize that it is impossible to find a perfect church to meet your entire family's needs. What you and your husband look for in a church may be very different. In the marriage chapter I talked about the need for evaluation and communication. In this decision you'll need both, with the realization that you may need to compromise.

When Dave and I chose our church, we did something quite unnatural. We decided to let God have the final say. First we did our part in checking out the programs, the doctrine, and the facilities. Then we asked for God's leading by praying specifically about which church to attend. We believed that He wanted the best for us. So we prayed until we both felt His peace about our decision. As a couple, we talked and found out that we both had peace about attending the same church.

God's leading can be trusted. Over the years that my husband and I have developed a relationship with God, we've come to trust Him for wisdom. I encourage you to do the same.

Boomeranging

"They're baaaaack," to quote a line from a movie that I never saw. That's what the oldsters are saying about us. We left the church and now we're back with our children. Even though time is precious and our other more urgent commitments beckon, we know that it's the right thing to do. And we're back in surprisingly big numbers. We have indeed boomeranged back to church. And for many of us, though not all of us, it is because we are moms.

Tess looked around for the others as coffee hour was coming to a close. She was on time, eager to go over the last minute details, as the other three eventually joined her.

Stacy started the informal meeting, "Let's get started. Tess, do you have the list?"

Tess already had it out and began with, "Only five more days until the young adult social for Friday night at church. How're the ticket sales and income?"

Stacy answered, "I'm disappointed. They are lower than I expected. I've been talking it up—I wanted this to be *the* event."

Tess added, "Well, then let's be careful how we spend money for the party."

Rachael offered, "Maybe some people don't know about the party. I'd love to call some—it'll be good to catch up with some people."

Tess said, "Good. Next, food and paper goods."

Ida piped up. "I'm trying some new recipes for fancy hors d'oeuvres and finger desserts. I've borrowed lacy tablecloths and silver candlesticks and floral napkins."

Rachael encouraged, "That sounds great. People will love it. But what about those who can't eat rich foods? I'd be glad to bring cut up fruit on toothpicks."

Ida nodded her head in agreement and added, "Served on silver trays, please."

Tess continued with, "Program/emcee/skit?"

Stacy said, "The skit is all set, more or less. I had to twist a few arms to get people to act in it. No problem with the program. Basically we'll start with an opening get to know each other game, followed by food, and then entertainment. I'll play it by ear for the length of each activity."

Tess asked, "What about the set-up at the church?"

Rachael answered, "I had a good talk with Tim, the custodian. He'll set up the round tables instead of chairs facing a stage. That way people can talk more in little groups."

Ida's thoughts wandered from the conversation as she pictured the party-to-be. Rachael would talk with most everybody there. Stacy would shine in her roles of emcee and star of the skit. Tess would fuss and worry about all of the details. People would enjoy the food and atmosphere courtesy of Ida. After all, this whole party had been her idea, and everyone seemed to enjoy her part of the planning.

As it turns out, the evening was a blast. Stacy was her promoting self in front of the group as emcee. Tess had every base covered—nothing was overlooked. The tables looked pretty; Ida had some good decorating ideas too. Rachael was the evening's table hopper. Ida met with some people about an hour beforehand to go over the skits. She had her part organized well and more or less relaxed the rest of the evening.

Church in the nineties.

PART EIGHT

Reviewing
Realistic Expectations

Chapter 14

Take Care

———————◆———————

"Take care" is the term the older generation in my family uses when we depart after a visit. As we are leaving, they give us hugs, smiles, and the charge: "Take care." As a youngster I thought the expression was strange; a little weird and corny. But now I've come to know that it is what my family does. And the meaning of "Take care," as spoken by members of my family, means more to me than good-bye or farewell or just about any other word for good-bye.

As reader and writer it's almost time for us to part ways. But I wanted to tell you not good-bye, but take care. Not because I know you personally, but because I know of you through the common struggles we share in the job of motherhood. As defined by *The American Heritage Dictionary*, take care means "to be careful." And "take care of" means "to assume responsibility for the maintenance, support, or treatment of."[1] So before we part ways, I'd like to take this time to review the Green Light Concept succinctly for you so that you will remember how to take care the GLC way. Because GLC takes into account who you are as a person and lets you fit the job of motherhood to you, you and your family will both be better cared for.

Status Quo for You

What is your fulfillment level as a mother right now? You can think of fulfillment levels as being like a gas tank. If you have more than half a tank, you're doing well. If you have less than that and you're not filling up your tank, you probably feel frustrated and stressed. You can replenish your gas tank by using activities and skills in your Green Focus area, and by pursuing your lifetime dreams. You don't let your car (or minivan) run out of gas, so don't allow yourself to either.

On a scale of 1 to 10, rate how satisfied and fulfilled your life is. Then check your number with the chart below.

0– 5   Caution; fill up your tank.

5– 7   Good steady-paced and balanced realistic lifestyle.

7–10   Excellent, nearly ideal fulfillment. Enjoy these times when they happen; you are in stride.

Satisfaction levels below a five are troublesome. Levels between five and seven are good, but leave room for improvement. Levels above seven are great and need no adjustments. What is your satisfaction level right now?

To help you evaluate your level of satisfaction, I've developed a list of typical jobs involved in mothering and how each one affects you depending on your Green Light Profile.

Each job is rated as a G (Green), Y (Yellow), or R (Red) for each Focus area (Strategy, Tasks, Relationships, Ideas). The ratings indicate what type of person is in his or her Green, Yellow, or Red Focus area while doing that particular job. For example, if you are a Strategy person, accompanying children is a Red for you. If you aren't sure of your Green Light Profile, look at the job, decide whether it is a Green, Yellow, or Red for you, and note which columns (Strategy, Tasks, Relationships, or Ideas) match.

Greens are jobs that you enjoy doing and do well. You may label a particular job as Yellow if you can do it for short periods of time or with average satisfaction and results. A Red means that too much time in that activity leads to frustration and stress because your performance and satisfaction levels are low.

The question is, "How can you fit the job of motherhood to you as a person with your particular Green Light Profile?" That question is especially critical if your fulfillment level is low and has been for a long time. If this is the case with you, you are probably frustrated and stressed. Now you know why.

How can these jobs be changed to fit who you are? Some jobs can be made more palatable by squeezing in some Greens while you do them.

Here are a few possibilities. If you are a Relationships mom, do unpalatable jobs with other people. If you are an Ideas mom, try to learn as you do Reds, and spend a lot of time teaching your children how to design and

Typical Jobs in Mothering (GLC Rating)

	Strategy	Tasks	Relationships	Ideas
Accompany children	R	R	G	R
Assembling things	R	G	R	R
Assisting kids	R	G	G	G
Baking creatively	R	R	R	G
Building relationship with husband	R	R	G	Y
Building relationship with children	R	R	G	Y
Budgeting	R	G	R	R
Cleaning	R	G	R	R
Coaching to develop a person	R	G	G	G
Cooking three meals a day	R	G	R	Y
Living a creative lifestyle	R	R	Y	G
Making decisions (the results)	G	R	R	R
Making decisions (the process)	R	G	R	G
Decorating the house	R	Y	Y	G
Designing and making clothes	R	Y	Y	G
Disciplining children with spanking	G	G	R	R
Disciplining children without spanking	R	R	G	Y
Living a disciplined lifestyle	G	G	R	R
Entertaining	R	R	G	Y
Running errands	R	Y	Y	R

Typical Jobs in Mothering (cont.)

	Strategy	Tasks	Relationships	Ideas
Fixing up the house	R	G	Y	Y
Setting goals with children	G	G	R	R
Inspiring children	G	R	R	R
Having friends over to play	R	R	R	R
Doing the minivan shuffle (running around, going places)	R	G	G	R
Operating a car or other vehicle	Y	G	R	R
Organizing a birthday party	R	G	G	R
Organizing the house	R	G	R	R
Planning vacations	G	G	R	R
Playing with children	R	R	G	R
Making repairs	R	G	R	R
Saving money	R	G	R	R
Sewing	R	Y	Y	G
Socializing	R	R	G	Y
Teaching	R	G	Y	G
Working together with husband	R	R	G	R
Training children	R	G	Y	Y
Going on vacation	R	R	G	G

do the job quickly to get on to other work. And if you are make things, as well as decorating your home. If you are a Strategy person, squeeze in some Greens by trying to a Tasks person, set up a system with standards, procedures, and checks and balances, and do each job by yourself, with no one around to interrupt you.

Another way to mix Greens with Reds is to avoid some jobs altogether. There are three possibilities that come to my mind here; perhaps you can think of others. The first is not to do the job at all. (Gasp!) In my house, we rarely make beds (yet the world hasn't stopped spinning). The second possibility is to have your husband or children do the job. Whoever is better designed than you to do the task could do it. You never know, it may even be in his or her Green. A third alternative to facing solid Reds is to hire help.

For peace of mind you can lower your standards for the jobs of motherhood that are in your Red areas. This means allowing yourself not to feel as though you must be perfect in everything you do. Give yourself a break; you're not meant to do or be everything.

I give myself breaks. For example, cleaning house is a Red. It involves no learning (a Green for me). Yet it must be done, for many reasons (sanitation, organization, social acceptability). If I were to grade myself on this job, I'd give myself about a C. That's not a good grade for someone used to getting mostly A's. Yet I don't belittle myself because my capabilities for housecleaning hover around a C. I do it because it must be done. I congratulate myself when I do it, realizing my low performance is in line with my abilities in this area. Remembering my Profile, my intrinsic design, alleviates stress. I remind myself that this is who I am. So remember to be kind to yourself and to evaluate the jobs of motherhood against who you are.

For those jobs that are a part of your Green, spend more time doing them and raise your expectations and standards for yourself in that job. For example, if you are an Ideas mom, you could spend more time designing, sewing, decorating, and baking, and a lot less time cleaning or organizing the house; you could also spend more time teaching your children outside in nature or at the library or a museum.

If you are a Tasks mom, you could spend more time on cleaning and organizing than on spending time with kids or decorating.

A Relationships mom could adjust her day toward Greens by spending most of her day with people and her children and a lot less time on cooking, cleaning, decorating, and organizing.

And if you are a Strategy person, you probably find very little fulfillment in homemaking; you will often be at a loss as to how to squeeze in Greens where there are so few fulfilling areas. One way you can adjust is to set an example consciously and be an inspiration to your children. You are a visionary and can inspire others, so you can help others to set goals for themselves, particularly useful in pursuing lifetime dreams. You'll need to use your Yellow Focus area to find fulfillment in your homemaker jobs. If you are a Strategy person, I suggest you reread the job listing above with your Yellow in mind.

Reevaluate

After you make some changes to your mothering tasks to reflect your Green Light Profile, reevaluate your fulfillment level or try to predict how your satisfaction will change. If your fulfillment level is still too low, there are at least two choices available to you:

1. Continue doing what you're doing because of a value judgment that you have made. For example, a

mother chooses to work at home full time until her children are in school. Even though her fulfillment level is lower than she'd like, she is willing to make this sacrifice during this time for her children. Her attitude will be better as she remembers that she has made her choice. The power of convictions and values is amazing.

2. Add a new activity or commitment that is solidly in your Green. Though you value time with your children, you feel that your current lifestyle is not working for you. Perhaps motherhood plus one other activity (or two) will help you make the job of motherhood fit who you are and raise your fulfillment level. This one activity, if solidly in your Green, can help reduce a lot of frustration. Right now you feel frustrated and want to make some changes. It may be time for you to make some adjustments to your lifestyle, such as:

- ◆ doing volunteer work
- ◆ pursuing a hobby
- ◆ working for pay outside of the house or in a home-based business
- ◆ taking classes to get training in your Green Action Skills

Seasons in Life that Make Us Want to Evaluate

As a mom, your life is intertwined with that of your children, and in a lot of instances their stage in life affects your life directly. The most clear-cut seasons listing I've found is from Chuck Swindoll, a pastor and author:

Stage 1: Family founding. This begins with the wedding and goes through the birth of the first child.

Stage 2: Childbearing. This starts with the birth of the first child and lasts until the last child enters school.

Stage 3: Child rearing. This lasts from the time the first child enters school until the last child enters college or leaves home.

Stage 4: Child launching. Beginning with the first child's departure from home, this stage lasts until the last child leaves.

Stage 5: Empty nest. All the children have left home now.[2]

All of these stages are good times to reevaluate your life as a person. All are particularly good times to examine your lifetime dream, because each of them represents more free time for you to pursue other activities.

Other women have made a time commitment to their families based on the above stages. These women have made a value judgment to look at their life with the long view in mind. Some women I know will not work for pay until their youngest child begins first grade. Still others have chosen not to work for pay until their youngest child leaves the nest (I definitely am not one of those women); those women are able to see that they have seventy-five years of life and are willing to devote ten, fifteen, twenty, or even more years exclusively to their families.

There are at least three possible outcomes to the decision to commit some period of time to the family. One is that "if her marriage is in good shape and her children are reasonably whole, a woman brings to this stage of her life tremendous drive and energy."[3] The second is that "the trouble with that kind of woman, of course, is that if you didn't stick around for a long time you'd miss the beauty of their performance."[4] Still a third outcome is that a single mom has reestablished and raised a healthy family despite the absence of a father; thus, she has energy to devote to a career.

Other opportune times to reevaluate are times of stress. You can feel stressed when you are too busy and too overcommitted. Stress is felt when you are frustrated a lot of the time. Stress increases when you are out of whack with your Profile and spending too little time within your Greens. Stress is prominent when you feel burned out, perhaps running around meeting other people's needs and virtually ignoring your own, when you are overloaded with personal or family crises.

Times of change can bring on opportunities for reevaluation. One such change is the birth of a new baby. No matter how many children you have, a little one will throw your balance out of balance for a while. Initially you may feel as though nothing is getting done. It takes your body time to heal, and it takes time for the baby to fit in with the rest of the family. Other changes may occur in the area of paid work and can affect your relationship with your husband. Work changes such as layoffs, transfers, and promotions cause times of immense change. Also, changes occur when you are asked to take on more responsibility in your work or volunteer work. Additional changes occur when your parents experience a prolonged illness or die; you then become the oldest generation.

Still other times for evaluation can come when you are feeling low. It may just be a time of "I feel like I'm just a mother." Those times could involve a lot of sleepless nights with sick children or could be as a result of having too many commitments and not having the energy to fulfill them all. Or they could be a mismatch between your capabilities and your responsibilities. You may need encouragement. You may feel unappreciated or uncared for (especially if you are a Relationships person).

How to Review

One of the biggest obstacles to reevaluating your life is convincing yourself that you need to set aside time to do it. You may think, *I'm so busy, so overwhelmed, how could I possibly set aside time now?* Yet it is vital for your own well-being. You need to get out of the whirlwind of life's activities in order to think and evaluate. You *need* to make time to evaluate.

So get away for an afternoon or a weekend, if at all possible, and do this:

1. Reread parts or all of this book as needed.

2. List all your responsibilities. Evaluate each one using the typical jobs in mothering chart in this chapter.

3. Keep in mind some key GLC principles:

The importance of pursuing a lifetime dream, a life purpose. Keep your lifetime dreams in mind as you come to an evaluation time in your life. The real you is what you envision when you can see beyond the dishes, the diapers, and the dailies. What is keeping you from pursuing what you really want? Begin today with one small step. Think of goals as the little steps to help you achieve your lifetime dream. A dream without goals is like a date night without communication.

Remember that your work has value. Throughout your life remember that all work has value whether paid or unpaid and whether esteemed by society or not. Society tends to value jobs with money and status. Are you to sigh and resign yourself to the influences of society? You must realize that all work is valuable when done with proper motives, when it is not illegal or immoral, and when it is done to the best of your abilities. And you must realize that you have a choice.

Find the right balance for your family. That choice is lived out in your priorities and values and can be seen in how you choose to spend your time. I referred to the family equation in Chapter Nine. The family equation asks, "How is each member of the family doing with all of the activities and responsibilities in our lives?" This equation takes into consideration each person of the family. Is each person given opportunity to discover or use his or her Greens? And through all of your busyness, does each family member receive acceptance, love, respect, and the freedom to grow and change? No one but your family can determine your family equation—not society, not peers, not extended family, and not the media. Only you and your family members can decide your family equation. And "the compositions we create in these times of change are filled with interlocking messages of our commitments and decisions."[5]

Be persistent. You'll have to be persistent when pursuing your lifetime dreams, for a number of reasons. First, as a woman many things can cloud your vision and derail you from pursuing them. Thus, you will have to say no, again and again, to some good opportunities in order to pursue the best ones. Second, there will always be pressure to be the Perfect Mother, and those pressures can keep you from pursuing your lifetime dreams. You'll fit in better with the job of motherhood if *you* write the job description. And lastly, lifetime dreams take so long to be accomplished that you may feel like giving up. Persevere. The pursuit of dreams brings personal fulfillment as well as the fruits of your labor. The Bible encourages us, "In due time we shall reap if we do not grow weary" (Galatians 6:9, NASB). So enjoy the process while keeping in mind the results.

4. There is more to life than the principles of the Green Light Concept. So don't forget the importance of your body and spirit. If you are overtired or overweight, your sense of fulfillment diminishes. Similarly, if your relationship with God is out of balance, you will be out of balance. I know in my own life that when my juggling act becomes overwhelming, I'll drop the ball in the body area to maintain the spirit. In the Phillips version of the Bible, "Bodily fitness has a certain value, but spiritual fitness is essential both for this present life and the life to come" (1 Timothy 4:8).

Can We Make Life Perfect?

You know the answer is no. There are too many variables beyond your control. The two variables that come to mind first are circumstances and unpredictable people. My family still runs out of milk and bread. Sometimes we run out of clean towels. So I try to make my goal contentment rather than perfection. William Hulmes recommends, "If you can accept your imperfection, you can learn to be content. . . ."[6] A realistic view of yourself and your abilities, along with finding a balance in your life that suits you and your family, helps in your quest for contentment. Don't expect yourself to be perfect. It takes a lot of valuable energy trying to play the perfect role. Judith Viorst wrote, "Everyone wants to be perfect . . . perfection is not possible in other areas of our life, so why do we keep believing that a good mother is always loving and understanding?"[7]

"HLP"

At the beginning of this book I mentioned a license

plate that read "HLP5KDS." I don't know you personally, the number of children in your family, your family
circumstances, or your personal struggles. But I hope
this was the help you were looking for in finding your
niche for the job of mothering. The Green Light Concept
has helped me take care of myself. Use it to help take care
of yourself.

Here are words that summarize *The Myth of the Perfect
Mother*: "She's working at something she loves to do, not
to be loved, not because someone else expects it, and not
because she'll feel bad if she doesn't. She knows that no
one can do everything and do it well and that there is
always a price to be paid for doing too much. She knows
how to relax and have fun—she doesn't have to be
perfect."[8]

The Green Light Concept has been and continues to
be the most practical help I have ever received in my
roles as a wife, mom, and woman. If you've been frustrated and stressed by trying to live up to the myth of the
perfect mother, why not concentrate on your uniqueness? After all, no mother is perfect, but every mother is
unique. Life is too precious and short for you to be
something you're not. My hope for you is that you will
have the courage to set realistic expectations for yourself
based on your Green Light Profile, Green Action Skills,
lifetime dreams, and personal values. I pray that you will
have the mature patience to enjoy where you are now, all
the while looking forward to the changes the future will
bring. Begin today with one small step: shatter the myth
of the Perfect Mother by developing your own mothering
niche and discovering the valuable person that you are.

Take care.

PART NINE

Appendices
Notes

Appendix A

GLC Focus Areas
Further Explained

Ideas

How you tend to function with other people:
Green = by yourself
Yellow = delegate to others, some prefer to work with people
Red = working with other people

How far you tend to plan ahead:
Green = one month to one year
Yellow = less than one month
Red = one year or more

How much information and/or evaluation you collected/did:
Green = collected lots of information; lots of analysis (some prefer to collect some information; some analysis)
Yellow = collected some information; some analysis
Red = sized up on the spot; no analysis

Pet peeves or work conditions that tend to bother you a lot:
- Asked to make decisions about results such as productivity and strategizing
- Not given enough time to visualize design and think through creatively
- Doing mechanical, routine tasks causes boredom and emotional letdown
- Lack of opportunity to discuss issues/concepts in-depth with associates
- Answers and results expected too soon, not time enough to learn and gain confidence

Ideal work conditions or where you grow best:
+ Much alone time where you use your brain, reflecting, reading, conceptualizing and researching
+ Need to be allowed creativity in ideas, approaches, techniques

+ Opportunity to come up with your own ideas, need to start project from the beginning
+ A learning environment where you can ask questions and learn continually
+ Your expertise is valued and people use your ideas
+ Opportunity to be around other learner type people for think tank sessions

Relationships

How you tend to function with other people:
Green = by yourself or with others (some function best with others)
Yellow = with other people or by yourself
Red = delegate to others

How far you tend to plan ahead:
Green = one month or less
Yellow = one month to one year
Red = more than one year

How much information and/or evaluation you collected/did:
Green = sized up on the spot; no analysis; rather intuition (some function best by collecting some information; some analysis)
Yellow = collected some information; some analysis (some size up on spot)
Red = collected lots of information; lots of analysis

Pet peeves or work conditions that tend to bother you a lot:
− In situations where people compete against or are isolated from one another
− Situations where "everyone" is expected to do the same function, with little opportunity for uniqueness, one of a kind
− Working for sales, profits, growth, and results
− With a critical boss who gives too much constructive criticism
− Lack of encouragement and positive comments

Ideal work conditions or where you grow best:
+ Your boss and peers respect and affirm you as a person and for your work; your supervisor knows how to encourage you
+ In situations where people function together as a team
+ Sense of helping people by counseling, advising, building relationships
+ Work in a stable and encouraging environment
+ Situations allowing individuality where you can let your personality be known

Strategy

How you tend to function with other people:
Green = by yourself (some function best by delegating)
Yellow = delegate to others
Red = working with other people

How far you tend to plan ahead:
Green = one month to one year (some function best over one year)
Yellow = one year or more
Red = less than one month

How much information and/or evaluation you collected/did:
Green = collected some information; some analysis (some function best with no analysis)
Yellow = sized up on the spot; no analysis
Red = collected lots of information; lots of analysis

Pet peeves or work conditions that will tend to bother you a lot
- Not given enough time beforehand to plan and set goals, therefore frustrated at what you are aiming for
- Too much time spent with people, affirming them and helping them
- Being unprepared and so looking bad in front of others
- Too much fierce competition or too little planning for an event
- Waiting for permission to make a decision, as from a board or another authority
- In situations where survival is not at stake and don't rock the boat situations

Ideal work conditions or where you grow best:
+ Need some risk to make it challenging but need time to plan, set goals, and strategize
+ Ability to see progress quickly (initially), throughout stages of project and particularly at the end
+ Situations where there are dire needs such as company will go bankrupt, problems are everywhere, and you make fast decisions
+ When in front of or in charge of others or while performing on stage
+ Situations where you can be decisive: sees situations as black or white, right or wrong, finished or unfinished.
+ Chance to beat your personal best, instead of competing directly with others

Tasks

How you tend to function with other people:
Green = by yourself
Yellow = delegate to others
Red = working with other people

How far you tend to plan ahead:
Green = one month or less
Yellow = one month to one year
Red = one year or more

How much information and/or evaluation you collected/did:
Green = collected lots of information; lots of analysis (some
    function best collecting and analyzing some information)
Yellow = collected some information; some analysis
Red = sized up on the spot; no analysis

Pet peeves or work conditions that tend to bother you a lot:
– No problems to be solved, nothing to be fixed
– Asked to make decisions about results such as productivity
  and strategizing
– Working with other people as part of a team
– A supervisor who is "always" looking over your shoulder
– Where you cannot be in control of your schedule and others
  around you
– Supervisor who wants you to just "do the job" and is not
  concerned about the details

Ideal work conditions or where you grow best:
+ Supervisor who will let you be careful, cautious and consistent
  in your work and decisions
+ Being a key resource with solutions, and making final decision
  as to problem resolution
+ Where you are in charge of everything to complete a job
  without getting others to help
+ Having time to work alone, collect lots of information and
  analyze a lot
+ Particularly likes to be a consultant, likes to be called in
+ Functioning with things that can be controlled and that are predictable; equipment, machines, trainable/controllable people,
  vehicles

Appendix B

Volunteer Opportunities, Hobbies, and Jobs Suited to Each GLC Focus Area

Each woman needs to match her skills from Chapter Three with a job occupation or a hobby. As you interview and investigate proposed or current opportunities, make sure your skills fit what the position requires. If the skills and fulfillment are a match, then you are likely to enjoy the position. If you do not have formal training but your skills match a position, you may have to think about getting formal training by school and experience. You can get formal training or experience through college level courses, adult education workshops, volunteer positions, internships, and specialized courses.

Some places and organizations that seek volunteers include: Schools, churches, libraries, elderly services, homes for the mentally ill, crisis pregnancy centers, organizations that settle foreign families, Habitat for Humanity, Ronald McDonald House, Special Olympics, homeless kids and families, Junior Achievement, nature centers, hospitals, literacy programs, mothers' support groups, nursing homes, scouting, soup kitchens, prisons, Big Sister programs.

Ideas

Occupations that may suit you:

Artist

Carpenter, specialty work, unique creations

Coach, to develop

Consultant

Designer

Detective

Engineer

Homemaker, decorating and creative cooking aspects of

Law enforcement

Lawyer

Medical

Negotiator

Nurse

Performer

Persuader/debater

Photographer

Psychologist

Researcher

Sewer of new and creative crafts, not routine piecework sewing

Supervisor

Teacher   Trainer
Technician   Writer

If you are an Ideas person whose skills involve learning, your responsibilities must allow you to be continually learning, using your mind actively. Possible home-based businesses include: consultant, researcher, tutor, writer. Volunteer possibilities include: tutor, coach to develop, researcher of information for an organization, grant writer for an organization, writer.

If you are an Ideas person whose skills involve making, creating, and building, you must be free to have time to think of creative new ideas and see them come to fruition. You like variety and uniqueness of design, so routine making of crafts for sale may tend to frustrate you. Possible home-based businesses include: artist, painter, clothes designer, specialty cook, specialty cake baker/decorator, floral arranger, custom gift basket maker, sewer, calligrapher, stenciler. Volunteer possibilities include: decorating committee, refreshments, sewing, crafts making or demonstrating, building houses with Habitat for Humanity.

Relationships
Occupations that may suit you:

Accompanist
Cashier, lots of people, interaction
Childcare
Consultant
Coordinator
Counselor
Driver
Exercise Instructor
Facilitator
Flight Attendant
Forest Ranger
Hairdresser
Homemaker, meeting the needs of children and husband

Modeling
Nurse
Performer
PR Representative
Psychologist
Salesperson, to help and assist (good at home-based, party sales)
Speaker
Supervisor, as part of team effort
Supporter/helper/encourager
Teacher
Travel Agent

Relationships people need to work directly with people, rather than things or data. Having a good boss and an affirming work environment is important. Possible home-based businesses include: counselor, tutor, daycare provider, travel agent. Volunteer possibilities include: Big Sister, friend for the mentally ill, helper of a pregnant teenage mom, counseling, childcare for a friend or for an organization, helper for a refugee family settling into the U.S., performer.

Strategy

Occupations that may suit you:

Athlete	Negotiator
Buyer	Performer
Coach, to win	Persuader
Director	Pilot
Firefighter	Promoter
Law Enforcement	Real Estate Speculator
Lawyer	Salesperson, lots of convincing
Manager	Speaker, to motivate, to challenge

A Strategy person's job must include challenge, risk, and competition. If you are a Strategy person, you need a job in which you can see measurable results. Possible home-based businesses include: sales, fundraiser and marketer. Volunteer opportunities include: help with Junior Achievement, coach, fundraiser, Board Member, event organizer, speaker, friend to those who need a friend but don't want a friend (kids in trouble with the law, pregnant teens, teens having trouble with their parents).

Tasks

Occupations that may suit you:

Bookkeeper	Lawyer
Budgeter, financial analysis	Machinist
Buyer	Mechanic
Car Repair	Nurse
Chimney Sweep	Pet Trainer
Consultant	Pilot
Counselor	Physical Therapist
Custodial, cleaning	Psychologist
Dental Hygienist	Researcher
Dentist	Secretary
Driver	Technician
Editor	Trainer
Engineer, problem solver	Typist
House restorer	

Tasks people must be enabled to have time to do their jobs completely and thoroughly to their satisfaction. They like to set up routines and standards and use these in their job to improve efficiency and cost. Possible home-based businesses include: bookkeeper, consultant, editing, mechanic, furniture refinishing and restoring, secretary, clothing alteration, furniture upholstery. Volunteer opportunities include: bookkeeper or treasurer, secretary, car mechanic, fixing houses and appliances, wallpapering and painting, cleaning.

Appendix C

Resources That Encourage Moms to Be Moms

To further encourage you in the job of mothering...

Focus on the Family
Colorado Springs, CO 80995
(719) 633-6287

Focus on the Family offers a monthly magazine that has relevant articles and that has details about their daily radio broadcast.

MOPS Int'l, Inc.
4175 Harlan Street
Suite 105
Wheat Ridge, CO 80033
(303) 420-6100

MOPS stands for Mothers Of PreSchoolers; this group can tell you about mother's support groups in your area.

Welcome Home
8310 A Old Courthouse Road
Vienna, VA 22182

This organization encourages mothers with their informative monthly magazine. The cost is $15 per year.

Home by Choice
P.O. Box 103
Vienna, VA 22183

Contact this organization for information about establishing or joining a mother's support group in your area.

Appendix D

Resources to Help Women in Paid Employment

Job Possibilities for Each GLC Profile

See Appendix B.

Job-hunting Strategies

Realize that, in terms of GLC Profiles, most people dislike the job-hunting process. Only some Strategy people enjoy the process of hard sell. Others do fine writing their resume (Ideas and Tasks) and interviewing (Relationships, Ideas, and Strategy), but few do well at selling themselves through discouraging circumstances. Being motivated to sell yourself in a tough job market is particularly difficult for Relationships people.

Resume-Writing Tips

Do the best you can do on your resume. Make sure that it is well organized, that it contains no typing errors, and that it is printed on good quality paper.

Include any relevant experience as a mom that would help in your target job. From the book *Back to Work* by Nancy Schuman and William Lewis comes the following suggestion for your resumé:

> You need to acquaint yourself with what career counselors call transferable skills. These are household skills which have a meaningful place in the work environment; they include financial planning, counseling, arbitration, negotiation, and delegation.[1]

Of course homemaking skills other than those listed above can be used in the world of paid work. Don't forget to mention volunteer work as you complete your resume. Again, from *Back to Work*, the following advice is important:

Employers are recognizing that volunteer commitments are "real" work. Think of the time and energy you have devoted through the years to your volunteer activities. Even if you were on committees, instead of leading them, you made some important contributions.[2]

The Interview

Before the interview, think through some important questions that you are likely to be asked. Some are illegal, but you may be asked them anyway. Think through your answers.

- ♦ Why do you want to return to work now?
- ♦ How have you kept current in your field or trained for this field?
- ♦ Have you made arrangements for child care?
- ♦ What are your back-up plans if the children are sick?
- ♦ How do you feel about leaving your children with a sitter while you work?
- ♦ Are you planning to get pregnant again?

Prepare for the interview by finding out about the company beforehand. Call someone you know who works there. Find out how large the company is by researching at the library (The Thomas Guide or other sources that the reference librarian suggests). Dress appropriately for the job during your interview. While most positions require conservative dress, artsy jobs do not. Once you land the job, you can tailor your wardrobe to the unwritten company dress code.

Here are some of my favorite questions to ask on a job interview. Remember, you are interviewing them too. Therefore, use the interview as an opportunity to learn about the job and the company. Use the information gained in an interview to analyze whether the position fits your Green Light Profile.

1. What are the four most time important job responsibilities in this position?
2. What percentage of my time would I give to each of these?
3. What kind of person would do this job well?
4. How will my supervisor function with me?

    5. How will my performance and my work be evaluated? How often? By whom?

    6. How does the organization plan?

    7. When and how often will I be expected to write plans and objectives for my work?

    8. How many hours per week is this position?

    9. What are your expectations about overtime?

    10. What questions do you have about my qualifications?

    11. When will you be making your hiring decision?

Be on time for the interview. Even better, be a few minutes early. Come prepared with information you will need to fill out the application form. Many companies require you to fill one out before an interview begins. For each of your previous jobs you will need information such as where you worked, your supervisor's name, your job responsibilities, length of employment, your reason for leaving, your rate of pay at the start and finish of your job, references, and educational training (where, when, and what courses and what degrees or certifications you received).

Do not be intimidated by the interviewer—you are both seeking information on which to base a decision. Be sure you learn the interviewer's name, and use it throughout the interview. Be an attentive listener. Answer questions thoroughly. Show your interest in the position by asking some of the questions above. At the end of the interview ask if the interviewer has any questions or if anything needs further clarification.

After the Interview

After the interview, review the job responsibilities and other information you've gathered. Compare the job with you and your GLC Profile. Does this job fit who you are? Evaluate the job to determine if it fits you.

After the interview, write a thank-you note to the interviewer. It will bring up your name one more time, and it's a thoughtful gesture. If you are not interested in the job, be sure to tell the interviewer this in your note. If you are interested, tell the interviewer so, and tell her why.

Resources to Help You Start Your Own Business

Some moms are able to work while their kids are around. But many more cannot. Many of us work-at-home for pay moms need to hire childcare or work while our husbands watch the kids or while they are asleep or at school.

I've been working at home for over three years. I offer these suggestions also:

- ♦ Meet clients somewhere for lunch to present a professional image
- ♦ Stick to your work schedule, even if housecleaning doesn't get done
- ♦ Have a separate work area
- ♦ Learn to say no; people may think your work schedule is negotiable because you work at home
- ♦ Have business cards and business stationery printed up if you need to advertise and promote your work
- ♦ Don't hesitate to use take-out meals and paper cups and plates when a deadline looms.

Mother's Home Business Network
P.O. Box 423
East Meadow, NY 11554
1-800-828-2259

Yearly membership is $25 (includes quarterly publication). Free brochure sent upon request.

The National Association for the Cottage Industry
P.O. Box 14850
Chicago, IL 60614
(312) 939-6490

Membership to this organization costs $45 per year. To receive information about this group, write to them and include a self-addressed stamped envelope. Also, include $3 to receive a sample copy of *The Cottage Connection*, their quarterly publication

Small Business Administration
1-800-827-5722 prerecorded message for information

Sources of Additional Training

Sometimes you may want to get additional training in order to apply for a particular job or for your own benefit and learning. The best advice is to get training specifically in your Green Focus area. Keep this in mind as you seek training. Education not only costs in money, but also valuable time. Here are places and ways to get additional training:

◆ Community colleges

◆ Colleges

◆ Evening classes

◆ Weekend seminars

◆ One-day seminars

◆ Recertification in your field

◆ Training from somebody already in that field, apprenticeship-style training

◆ Internships

◆ Volunteer activities

◆ Learn on your own by reading and doing and trying it, especially current information in your field of study (periodicals and research papers)

Appendix E

GLC Trained Counselors

If you would like to find out more about the Green Light Concept or have a person trained in GLC evaluate your Green Light Profile, contact Richard Hagstrom for further information. He can be reached at this address:

Hagstrom Consulting, Inc.
83 Barrie Road
East Longmeadow, MA 01028

Please enclose a self-addressed stamped envelope.

Appendix F

For Further Reading

Chapters 1 and 2

The New Mother's Guide, by Ruth Alig and Stephanie Wright
And Then I Had Kids, by Susan Yates
The Myth of the Bad Mother, by Jane Swiggart
Husband Is the Past Tense of Daddy, by Teryl Zarnow

Chapter 4

What you read concerning your lifetime dream depends upon what motivates you to pursue it. You can read or learn from biographies, real-life role models, and from books on pursuing your particular dream.

I also recommend *I Wish I Had a Big, Big Tree,* by Satous Sato and Tsutomu Murakami.

Chapter 5

The Marriage Builder, by Larry Crabb, Ph.D.
Building Your Mate's Self Esteem, by Dennis and Barbara Rainey
The Myth of the Greener Grass, by J. Allan Petersen
Passive Men, Wild Women, by Pierre Mornell, M.D.
You Just Don't Understand, by Deborah Tannen

Chapter 6

And Then I Had Kids, by Susan Yates
Motivating Your Kids from Crayons to Career, by Cheri Fuller
The New Mother's Guide, by Ruth Alig and Stephanie Wright
What Kids Need Most in a Mom, by Patricia H. Rushford

Chapter 7

One on the Seesaw, by Carol Lynn Pearson
Single Parenting, by Robert G. Barnes, Jr.

Chapters 9 and 10

The Part-Time Solution, by Charlene Canape
Back to Work—How to Reenter the Working World, by Nancy Schuman
and William Lewis
Getting Along with Yourself and Others: The art of solving people problems,
by Richard G. Hagstrom

Chapter 12

Between Walden and the Whirlwind, by Jean Fleming
Disciplines of the Beautiful Woman, by Anne Ortland
Hope Has Its Reasons, by Rebbeca Pippert

Appendix G

GLC Discovery Guide

Positive Experiences Listing

Write down the 14 most positive experiences you've had. Positive experiences are activities that you did well and which gave you a sense of satisfaction. Describe 7 from age 5 to halfway to your present age, and 7 from the second half of your life.

Time Period I—first half of your life

1.

2.

3.

4.

5.

6.

7.

Time Period II—second half of your life

1.

2.

3.

4.

5.

6.

7.

Examples of Positive Experiences

Here are some examples of positive experiences.

Time Period I

♦ Age 9, campaigned for local politician

♦ Sold books door-to-door, sold cookies the next year

♦ Gave speech to 400 people

♦ Coached winning teams

♦ Successfully directed the turnaround of a failing business; now rapidly growing

♦ Read over 900 books before age 12

♦ Drew wildlife scenes

♦ Wrote articles and short stories

♦ Invented and designed two new products

♦ Took advanced math and physics; taught these to other students

Time Period II

♦ Organized stock room (made it neat and orderly)

♦ Office administrator—handled paperwork

♦ Did problem solving with people; advised them based on data

♦ Trained people to use office equipment

♦ Built models from kits; made scaled down furniture too

♦ Took family vacations; enjoyed traveling together, being together

♦ Made special gifts for people; also, "designed" the school bulletin board

♦ Counseled troubled people

♦ Coordinated special events/occasions, like a weekend retreat or an anniversary party

♦ Enjoyed softball and sorority; made a lot of friends

A. What You Did

For each of your positive experiences, write the letter (**S** for Strategy, **T** for Tasks, **I** for Ideas, **R** for Relationships) which best represents what you did. Refer to the chart that follows for a description of each category.

Time Period I

Positive Experience 1: _____

Positive Experience 2: _____

Positive Experience 3: _____

Positive Experience 4: _____

Positive Experience 5: _____

Positive Experience 6: _____

Positive Experience 7: _____

Time Period II

Positive Experience 1: _____

Positive Experience 2: _____

Positive Experience 3: _____

Positive Experience 4: _____

Positive Experience 5: _____

Positive Experience 6: _____

Positive Experience 7: _____

Strategy

- directing
- selling with convincing
- competing
- speaking

Tasks

- organizing or maintaining
- repairing or building
- operating or controlling
- troubleshooting or training

Ideas

- researching
- writing or teaching
- designing
- producing/performing

Relationships

- visiting or building relationships
- coaching or teaching
- counseling or encouraging
- coordinating or PR representative

B. What You Thought

For each of your positive experiences, write the letter which best represents what you thought while doing it. Refer to the chart that follows for a description of each category.

Time Period I

Positive Experience 1: _____

Positive Experience 2: _____

Positive Experience 3: _____

Positive Experience 4: _____

Positive Experience 5: _____

Positive Experience 6: _____

Positive Experience 7: _____

Time Period II

Positive Experience 1: _____

Positive Experience 2: _____

Positive Experience 3: _____

Positive Experience 4: _____

Positive Experience 5: _____

Positive Experience 6: _____

Positive Experience 7: _____

Strategy

How can I

- win?
- compete best?
- gain people's backing?

Tasks

What can I do to

- make it better?
- improve it?
- keep things running smoothly?

Ideas

I pondered how I could

- get complete understanding
- express it creatively
- make others understand

Relationships

I thought about who

- needed encouragement
- needed help
- needed a listening ear

C. What You Gave

For each of your positive experiences, write the letter which best represents what you contributed or passed on while doing it. Refer to the chart that follows for a description of each category.

Time Period I

Positive Experience 1: _____

Positive Experience 2: _____

Positive Experience 3: _____

Positive Experience 4: _____

Positive Experience 5: _____

Positive Experience 6: _____

Positive Experience 7: _____

Time Period II

Positive Experience 1: _____

Positive Experience 2: _____

Positive Experience 3: _____

Positive Experience 4: _____

Positive Experience 5: _____

Positive Experience 6: _____

Positive Experience 7: _____

Strategy

I contributed or passed on

- organizational growth or profits
- strategies to compete and win
- more adherents

Tasks

I contributed or passed on

- neatness and orderliness
- correctly completed job
- efficient solution

Ideas

I contributed or passed on

- new ideas and concepts
- new designs
- new products

Relationships

I contributed or passed on

- encouragement
- personalized, unique help
- concern and care

D. Tally the Results

Now tally the results of your exercise. Count the number of times each letter appears above, and write the totals here:

S: _____

T: _____

I: _____

R: _____

_____ Which letter appeared most often? This is your Green Focus area.

_____ Which letter appeared next most often? This is your Yellow Focus area.

_____ Which letter appeared least or not at all? This is your Red Focus area.

Your GLC Profile, or Effectiveness Profile, is comprised of your Green Focus area and your Yellow Focus area.

- ◆ **S** is for Strategy: the bottom line is results through strategizing.
- ◆ **T** is for Tasks: enjoys the process of working with details to obtain results.
- ◆ **I** is for Ideas: thrives on using ideas creatively either for the joy of learning or for creative, artistic expressions.
- ◆ **R** is for Relationships: loves spending time with people, known as "people people."

Notes

I am grateful to Hagstrom Consulting, Inc., for use of Green Light Concept material throughout *The Myth of the Perfect Mother*.

Chapter 1: The Myth of the Perfect Mother
1. Claudio Bepko and Jo-Ann Kreston, *Too Good for Her Own Good: Breaking Free from the Burden of Female Responsibility* (New York: Harper & Row Publishers, 1990), p. 7.

Chapter 2: Every Mother Is Unique
1. Nina Barrett, *I Wish Someone Had Told Me* (New York: Simon and Schuster, 1990), p. 3.
2. Jane Swiggart, *The Myth of the Bad Mother: The Emotional Realities of Mothering* (New York: Doubleday, 1991), p. 10.

Chapter 3: Mothering Styles
1. Walt Disney, *Alice in Wonderland*, directed by Clyde Geronomi, Hamilton Luske, and Wilfred Jackson (United States, 1951).
2. Tim Kimmel, *Little House on the Freeway* (Portland, OR: Multnomah Press, 1987), pp. 140-141.
3. Ruth Alig and Stephanie Wright, *The New Mothers Guide: Sorting Out Your Physical, Psychological, and Spiritual Changes in the First Twelve Months of Motherhood* (Colorado Springs, CO: NavPress, 1988), p. 151.

Chapter 4: Dream Makers
1. Satoru Sato and Tsutomu Murakami (English text by Hitomi Jitodai and Carol Eisman), *I Wish I Had a Big, Big Tree* (New York: William Morrow & Co., Inc., 1989).
2. Ibid.
3. *American Heritage Dictionary*, edited by William Morris (Boston, MA: Houghton Mifflin Company, 1976), s.v. dream.
4. Walt Disney, *Cinderella*, directed by Wilfred Jackson, Hamilton Luske and Clyde Geronomi (United States, 1950).
5. Carl Sandburg, in John Bartlett, *Bartlett's Familiar Quotations*, Fifteenth and 125th Anniversary Edition, edited by Emily Morison Beck et al. (Boston, MA: Little, Brown and Company, 1985), p. 761.
6. Ibid., quote by Aristotle, p. 86.
7. Ibid., p. 25.
8. Ibid., quote by Edgar Allen Poe, p. 526.
9. TCF/Allied Stars/Enigma, *Chariots of Fire*, produced by David Putnam (Great Britain, 1981).
10. David Henry Thoreau, in John W. Gardener, ed., *Quotations of Wit and Wisdom* (New York: W.W. Norton & Company, Inc., 1975), p. 50.
11. John Mason Brown, Ibid., p. 53.
12. Disney, *Cinderella*.
13. George Bernard Shaw, in Bartlett, *Bartlett's Familiar Quotations*, p. 681.
14. Montaigne, in Gardener, ed., *Quotations of Wit and Wisdom*, p. 59.
15. Warner Communications Company, *The NeverEnding Story*, directed by Wolfgang Petersen and Herman Weigel, Munich, © 1984 by Neue Constantin Film Productions Gmb.H..
16. Samuel Butler, in Gardener, ed., *Quotations of Wit and Wisdom*, p. 31.
17. Thomas A. Edison, *The Oxford Dictionary of Quotations*, second edition (New York: Oxford University Press, 1953), p. 195.
18. Theodore C. Sorensen, *Kennedy* (New York: Harper & Row Publishers, Inc., 1965), p. 594.
19. James Dobson, Ph.D., *Parenting Isn't for Cowards* (Waco, TX: Word Book Publishers, 1987), p. 189.
20. Sato and Murakami, *I Wish I Had a Big, Big Tree*.
21. Lao-tzu, Chinese philosopher, in Bartlett, *Bartlett's Familiar Quotations*, p. 65.
22. Pat Cahill, "Composing a Life," *The Springfield Sunday Republican*, Living Section, September 1, 1991, pp. F-1 and F-6.

Chapter 5: His Needs or Her Needs?
1. Susie Pearson, "Diana: What She's Learned, What She's Lost," *Ladies Home Journal*, June 1991, p. 196.
2. Mona Hodgson, "10 Ways Wives Can Say 'I Love You'," *Focus on the Family* Magazine, June 1991, p. 11.
3. Based on the work of Martin Blinder, M.D., "What If You and Your Husband Have Become Strangers?" *First Magazine*, April 15, 1991, p. 48.
4. J. Allan Petersen, *The Myth of the Greener Grass* (Wheaton, IL: Tyndale House Publishers, 1983), p. 73.
5. Carole Mayhill, *Marriage Takes More Than Love* (Colorado Springs, CO: NavPress, 1978), pp. 40-41.
6. Charles Churchill, *The Oxford Dictionary of Quotations*, p. 143.
7. James Dobson, Ph.D., *What Wives Wish Their Husbands Knew About Women* (Wheaton, IL: Tyndale House Publishers, Inc., 1975), p. 185.
8. Bill Cosby, *Love and Marriage* (New York: Doubleday, 1989), p. 108.
9. Deborah Tannen, Ph.D., *You Just Don't Understand* (New York: William Morrow & Company, Inc., 1990), p. 298.
10. Larry Crabb, Ph.D., *The Marriage Builder* (Grand Rapids, MI: Zondervan Publishing House, 1982), p. 64.
11. Frank and Sharan Barnet, *Working Together Entrepreneurial Couples* (Berkeley, CA: Ten Speed Press, 1988), p. 92.
12. Sandra Sohn Jaffe and Jack Vietrel, *Becoming Parents* in Beppe Harrison, *The Shock of Motherhood* (New York: Charles Scribner's Sons, 1986), p. 84.
13. Susan Alexander Yates, *And Then I Had Kids: Encouragement for Mothers of Young Children* (Brentwood, TN: Wolgemuth & Hyatt Publishers, Inc., 1988), p. 29.
14. Charles Churchill, *The Oxford Dictionary of Quotations*, p. 143.
15. *The International Dictionary of Thought*, compiled by John P. Bradley et al. (Chicago: J.G. Ferguson Publishing Company, 1969), p. 455.
16. Cosby, *Love and Marriage*, dedication page.
17. Chuck Swindoll, *Growing Wise in Family Life* (Fullerton, CA: Insight for Living, 1988), p. 163.
18. Anna Louise de Stael, *Dictionary of Quotable Definitions*, edited by Eugene E. Brussell (Englewood Cliffs, NJ: Prentice-Hall, Inc., 1970), p. 345.
19. Cosby, *Love and Marriage*, p. 135.
20. *Proverbs and Epigrams* (Ottenheimer, MCMLIV), p. 29.
21. Harville Hendrix, Ph.D., "10 Secrets of a Happy Marriage," *Family Circle Magazine*, February 19, 1991, p. 28.
22. Gerald G. Jampolsky, M.D., *One Person Can Make a Difference* (New York: Bantam, 1990), p. 153.
23. Jean Ingelow, *The Oxford Dictionary of Quotations*, p. 267.
24. Dobson, *What Wives Wish*, p. 186.

Chapter 6: Every Child a Surprise
1. Dobson, *What Wives Wish*, p. 145.
2. Proverbs 22:6, New American Standard Bible, Red Letter Edition, paragraphed (Philadelphia: A.J. Holman Company, 1977).
3. Richard G. Hagstrom, *Getting Along with Yourself and Others: The Art of Solving People Problems* (Wheaton, IL: Tyndale House Publishers, Inc., 1982), p. 164.
4. *American Heritage Dictionary*, s.v. project.
5. Larry Crabb, Ph.D., *The Marriage Builder* (Grand Rapids, MI: The Zondervan Corporation, 1982), p. 28.
6. Dr. Brazelton, *Working and Caring* (Reading, MA: Addison-Wesley Publishing, 1985), p. 12.
7. Marjorie Holmes, *Hold Me Up a Little Longer, Lord* (Garden City, NY: Doubleday & Company, Inc., 1977), p. 67.
8. Teryl Zarnow, *Husband Is the Past Tense of Daddy* (Reading, MA: Addison-Wesley Publishers, 1990), p. 133.
9. H. Norman Wright, "When Mom Is a Perfectionist," *Focus on the Family* Magazine, August 1991, p. 3.
10. Bill Cosby, *Fatherhood* (Garden City, NY: A Dolphin Book, Doubleday & Company, Inc., 1986), p. 95.
11. Robert G. Barnes, Jr., *Confident Kids* (Wheaton, IL: Tyndale House Publishers, Inc., 1987), p. 101.
12. Susan Alexander Yates, *And Then I Had Kids: Encouragement for Mothers of Young Children* (Brentwood, TN: Wolgemuth & Hyatt Publishers, Inc., 1988), p. 125.

13. Linda Burton, Janet Dittmer, and Cheri Loveless, *What's a Smart Woman Like You Doing at Home?* (Washington, D.C.: Acropolis, 1986), p. 87.
14. Kimmel, *Little House on the Freeway*, p. 182.

Chapter 7: If You Are Single

1. Hank Hersch, "Ace of the Angels," *Sports Illustrated*, September 9, 1991, p. 24.
2. Ibid., p. 22.
3. Ibid., p. 24.
4. Karen Levine, "Single... with Children," *Parents* Magazine, December 1990, p. 73.
5. Michael Blumenthal, "A Courage Born of Broken Promises," *New York Times Magazine*, July 23, 1989, p. 14.
6. Carol Lynn Pearson, *One on the Seesaw* (New York: Random House, 1988), p. 103.
7. Ibid., p. 113.
8. Robert S. Weiss, *Marital Separation* (New York: Basic Books, Inc., 1975), p. 74.
9. Charles Swindoll, *Improving Your Serve* (Waco, TX: Word, 1981), pp. 182-183.
10. Joan Anderson, *The Single Mother's Book* (Atlanta: Peachtree Publishers Ltd., 1990), p. 6.
11. Robert G. Barnes, Jr., *Single Parenting* (Wheaton, IL: Tyndale House Publishers, Inc., 1987), p. 9.
12. Blumenthal, "A Courage Born," p. 14.
13. Barnes, *Single Parenting*, p. 16.
14. Anderson, *The Single Mother's Book*, p. 136.
15. Sara Arline Thrash, *Dear God, I'm Divorced* (Grand Rapids, MI: Baker Book House, 1991), p. 12.
16. *Ibid.*, p. 90.
17. Susan Zitzman, "A Fork in the Road," *Christian Parenting Today*, March/April 1991, p. 55.
18. Dr. Fitzhurgh Dodson, *How to Single Parent* (New York: Harper & Row Publishers, 1987), p. 35.
19. Kathleen McCoy, *Solo Parenting: Your Essential Guide* (New York: New American Library, 1987), p. 12.
20. Patricia A. Bigliardi, "A Time for Two," *Focus on the Family* Magazine, December 1991, p. 4.
21. Anderson, *The Single Mother's Book*, p. 95.
22. Carol Lynn Pearson, *One on the Seesaw*, p. 11.
23. Ibid., p. 104.
24. Hersch, "Ace of the Angels," p. 22.

Chapter 8: A Clean Sweep

1. Patricia H. Rushford, *What Kids Need Most in a Mom* (Old Tappan, NJ: Fleming H. Revell Company, 1986), pp. 180-181.
2. Michelle Morris, "What Causes Stress, What Doesn't," under "How Is Your Work Affecting Your Health, Your Family, Your Life?" *McCall's*, March 1991, p. 76.
3. Elaine Fantle Shimberg, *How to Be a Successful Housewife/Writer: Bylines and Babies Do Mix* (Cincinnati: Writer's Digest Books, 1979), p. 60.
4. Ibid., p. 61.

Chapter 9: What Works for You

1. *Thirtysomething*, American Broadcasting Company, Marshall Herskovitz and Edward Zwick, 1990.
2. Pierre Mornell, M.D., *Passive Men, Wild Women* (New York: Ballantine Books, 1979), p. 82.
3. Internal Revenue Service, *1040 Forms and Instructions*, 1988 edition, pp. 14, 18.
4. *Working Mother*, May 1991, p. 8.
5. First Timothy 6:7, J.B. Phillips, The New Testament in Modern English, Revised Edition (New York: Macmillan Publishing Co., Inc., 1972).
6. *Thirtysomething*, 1990.

Chapter 10: What's a Mother to Do?

1. *Parent's* Magazine, June 1990 and July 1990.
2. Margery D. Rosen, "The American Mother: a landmark survey for the 1990's May 1990," *Ladies Home Journal*, pp. 132-136.
3. *Parent's* Magazine, June 1990, p. 108.
4. Zarnow, *Husband Is the Past Tense*, p. 103.
5. Tony Campolo, *20 Hot Potatoes Christians Are Afraid to Touch* (Waco, TX: Word Inc., 1988), p. 50.
6. Edith Fierst, "Careers and Kids," *MS*, May 1988, pp. 62, 64.

7. Phyllis Battelle, "Women's Lib Made Me Feel Inadequate and Useless," *Woman's Day*, October 30, 1990, p. 103.
8. *Family Circle* Magazine, June 27, 1989, p. 9.

Chapter 11: When to Say No
1. John Donne, *The Oxford Dictionary of Quotations*, p. 186.
2. Sally Shann, "Why Moms Need Good Friends," *Parents* Magazine, March 1991, p. 82.
3. Jean Fleming, *Between Walden and the Whirlwind* (Colorado Springs: NavPress, 1985), p. 17.
4. Dr. Jerry White, "Building Vision," Navigator conference, Colorado Springs, CO, October 2, 1989.

Chapter 12: Moms Have Other Needs Too
1. James Dobson, Ph.D., *Focus on the Family Bulletin*, June 1991, p. 1.
2. Natalie Angier, "Surprising Facts About Sleep," *Readers Digest*, June 1991, p. 33.
3. "Some People Are Born to Yo-Yo," *People Magazine*, January 13, 1992, p. 75.
4. Shakespeare, in *The Oxford Dictionary of Quotations*, p. 468.
5. Hugo de Anima, as quoted in *The Cyclopedia of Practical Quotations*, edited by J.K. Hoyt (New York: Funk and Wagnalls Co., 1886), p. 297.
6. Richard Chenevix Trench as quoted in *The Cyclopedia of Practical Quotations*, p. 522.
7. *Family Circle*, June 27, 1989, p. 9.
8. Rebecca Manley Pippert, *Hope Has Its Reasons: From the Search for Self to the Surprise of Faith* (San Francisco: Harper & Row Publishers, 1989), p. 98.

Chapter 13: Boomeranging Back to Church
1. "A Time to Seek," *Newsweek*, December 17, 1990, p. 51.
2. Paul C. Light, *Baby Boomers* (New York: W.W. Norton and Company, 1988), p. 24.
3. "Is Greed Dead?" *Fortune*, August 14, 1989, p. 41.
4. Quentin J. Schultze, "The Wireless Gospel," *Christianity Today*, January 15, 1988, p. 20.
5. "A Time to Seek," p. 52.
6. Bernice Kanner, "The Cadillac Straddle," *New York Magazine*, September 10, 1984, p. 23.
7. David Veerman, *How to Raise Christian Kids in a Non-Christian World* (Wheaton, IL: Victor Books, 1988), p. 77.

Chapter 14: Take Care
1. *American Heritage Dictionary*, s.v. take.
2. Swindoll, *Growing Wise*, pp. 115-116.
3. Brenda Hunter, *Home By Choice* (Portland, OR: Multnomah Press, 1991), p. 203.
4. Mary Murray Willison, *Diary of a Divorced Mother* (Ridgefield, CT: Wyden Books [div. of P.E.I. Bks.], 1980), p. 228.
5. Mary Catherine Bateson, *Composing a Life* (New York: A Plume Book, 1989), p. 241.
6. Alig and Wright, *The New Mothers Guide*, p. 151.
7. Judith Viorst, "What's the Best Advice You Can Give New Moms," *Redbook*, May 1990, p. 43.
8. Bepko and Kreston, *Too Good for Her Own Good*, p. 80.

Appendices
1. Nancy Schuman and William Lewis, *Back to Work* (Woodbury, NY: Barron's, 1985), p. 27.
2. Ibid., p. 63.